Spiritual Connections

Bringing to consciousness our spiritual interconnectedness

Written in short articles

Jack Schouten

Spiritual Books

First published in Australia in 1996 by
Spiritual Books
P.O.Box 8282 Wooloongabba Qld 4102

National Library of Australia
Cataloguing in Publication data

Schouten, Jack
Spiritual Connections: bringing to consciousness
our spiritual interconnectedness.

ISBN 0 646 29178 5.

1. Consciousness. 2. Spiritual life-New Age movement.
3. Mysticism.   I. Title.

Layout in Garamond 11pt. by Rafael and Jack Schouten
Cover Graphics and advice by Graphic Force
Printed in Australia by Griffin Paperbacks, Marion Road, Netley, SA
Cover Painting 'Reaching for the Sky' by Jack Schouten

        This book is dedicated to everyone who has assisted,
whether physically or spiritually. I particularly wish to thank
Heather Bell for all she did, and my sons Duncan and
Rafael Schouten.

TABLE OF CONTENTS

PREFACE 6

GLOSSARY 10

OUR NATURAL SPIRITUAL ACTIVITIES.

1. Implications of spiritual awareness. 35
2. Spiritual forces of nature and of humanity 41
3. Our personally created spiritual forces. 43
4. Our unconscious forces and their spiritual activity 45
5. Our supraconsciousness. 49
6. Our natural spiritual abilities. 51

INTUITIVE LIFE-FORCES FLOWING THROUGH A COMMUNITY.

7. Life forces flowing through a community 56
8. Indications of the flow of spiritual influence. 60
9. Different groups and different pathways for the flow 63
10. The awakening of independence in changing the flow 64
11. Indirect and random flows in a community 68
12. Interacting with the flow of life forces through us. 70
13. Bringing the flow to consciousness. 72

CONNECTIONS AS PATHWAYS FOR THE FLOW.

14. What are spiritual connections 75
15. Our intuitive selection of spiritual influences 80
16. Our historical connections with our families. 83
17. Connections through resonance with our soul qualities. 86
18. Connections through a common focus of attention. 88
19. Connections to physical objects. 91
20. Flows through our connections to physical objects. 93

EXPLORING THE FLOW WITHIN AND BETWEEN
INDIVIDUALS.

21. Our spiritual bodies.   97
22. The relationship of our spiritual bodies to each other   101
23. Altering our spiritual bodies.   104
24. Our etheric body and health.   107
25. The flow of spiritual forces between people   111

THE FLOW OF LIFE-ENERGY.

26. The flow of life-energy between our spiritual bodies   120
27. Sharing out life-energy amongst people   123
28. Negotiating the flows of life-energy.   126
29. Effects of concentrating and relaxing   129
30. Games people play to get a greater share of the flow   133
31. Leaders directing the flow   136
32. Letting go of fear and creating abundance.   138
33. Choosing to share the flow   142

BEING CHALLENGED BY THE INTUITIVE FORCES.

34. Being organized by the flow   146
35. Illness and crime as expressions of imbalance in the flow 147
36. Intuitive forces expressed through children   152
37. Community influences and the individual.   153
38. Being directed by our groupsoul   155
39. Being dominated by our groupmind.   157
40. Possession by an individual.   159
41. Collective patterning and the reoccurrence of events   162

BALANCING OUR PARTICIPATION IN THE FLOW.

42. Balancing our spiritual connections. 167
43. Coming to harmony after transitions 173
44. Supporting someone who is possessed 175
45. Unfolding our own destinies 179
46. Uncovering our Souls 181
47. Strengthening and balancing our Egos. 185
48. Discovering our Selves 188

CONSIDERING OUR CONNECTIONS IN DIFFERENT SITUATIONS.

49.Feeling out our connections when meeting people. 193
50.Acting with the support of a group. 196
51.Creating new spiritual connections. 197
52.Becoming an individual through diverse connections. 200
53 Initial imbalances in new connections. 203
54 Reasons we may feel the spiritual presence of people 205
55 Entering a building or village. 209
56 Creating our own space 213
57 Taking over someone's role. 216
58 Being connected to our community. 218

NATURAL USES OF THE FLOW THROUGH OUR CONNECTIONS.

59. Creation with our minds 222
60. Parents as spiritual guides of their children 224
61. Teachers guiding their pupils spiritually 228
62. Using our connections for spiritual healing 233
63. Healing and creating harmony through a group. 237
64 .Healing the energy of a place. 239
65. Healing with stories and myths. 241
66. Cooperative creation of future events 245
67. Mutual empowerment of future events 247
68. About using Spiritual guidance. 248

PREFACE

In writing this book I hope to enable an attitude of relaxed, but awakened, appreciation of other realms, our human spiritual natures and our normal, personal, spiritual activities. I am confining myself to human spiritual forces as these influence most of the changes in our lives.

Our spiritual nature asserts itself on the world in an individual way in an attempt to make the world into our own image. Each change in us alters the forces we impose on the world. Everyone else is also being spiritually assertive and gradually changing due to the spiritual or physical interactions they are involved in.

In having moments of spiritual perception, such as visions, out of body experiences, telepathy, intuitions, premonitions and inspirations, or in parts of dreams, everyone can get glimpses of their human spiritual activity and the potential for more of it to become conscious.

When we are spiritually conscious, we are usually limited to a few possibilities. Our potential however, as indicated by the totality of what is commonly experienced by different people, is far greater. We are all able to perceive any possible experience of life that we have an interest in, at any moment in the future or past, distant place or different realm, here and now if we can link our minds and spirits to it. Just as we can be limited in how many places on earth we visit and in how many things we see and do in a lifetime in the physical realm, our consciousness is also limited in spiritual realms. The most clairvoyant or spiritually awake people can only be aware of a fraction of what they are involved in or that affects them. We can trust that our intuitive aspects, our community or the cosmos, will take care of all that remains unconscious to us.

It is possible to consider all spiritual activity as minor adjuncts to our physical life, but my spiritual experience teaches me that changes in the physical world are manifestations of our activities in spiritual realms.

Mankind, as a whole, has developed far enough for many people to be secure in their personal foundations, or self knowledge. They can allow spiritual forces to come to consciousness in them again, while keeping their individuality and sanity intact, using discernment to choose whether or how to be influenced.

It is within our potential to direct our thoughts, emotions and imaginations as we choose. Our spiritual perception is already occurring naturally but we only bring a fraction of it to consciousness as all of our attention is usually needed by our daily tasks.

It is easy to forget or deny our spiritual activities and spare ourselves the initial complications of opening up to spiritual realms and realities. As with any new field of endeavour, coming to familiarity and consciousness in spiritual activities, is a demanding one.

If we can acknowledge ourselves as spiritual beings, we may also gradually accept responsibility for our spiritual activities. These continue every moment, and can be added to or reorganized with our every thought and desire, whether we acknowledge it or not.

I have consciously experienced everything I write about in some way myself, some of it daily and others, as can be expected from the amount of material I cover, only occasionally. There is still much for me to explore.

Occasionally, in my own life, I choose and initiate new spiritual possibilities, often I allow my existing karmic forces to complete themselves but usually I am caught up in the events being created by other people, just as we all are. At these times I can spiritually observe and learn, cooperate with the unfolding of the communities forces or choose to assert myself. My own understanding has gradually unfolded in this way.

Spiritual development is a personal affair. We can discuss and share all that we discover but essentially we learn through our own experiences which become possible as a natural result of the appropriate development of our bodies, souls and minds.

In this book I attempt to enable a broad understanding of spiritual activity rather than offer techniques. I have found that ignorance, disbelief, guilt about our spiritual creations, and fear, are the biggest barriers to spiritual consciousness. In coming to accept spiritual activities as normal, and ourselves as fallible, we also allow ourselves to be more perceptive and conscious in them.

By observing ourselves, the world around us and our thoughts, feelings and impulses, and noticing their connections, patterns and relationships, we can begin today, to perceive the spiritual forces at work. This will lead to new types of perception and an understanding of our ability to create spiritually.

While I do my best to be accurate and truthful, my understanding and interpretation can be questioned at times, so this book needs to be explored and questioned rather than simply accepted. Rather than waiting till I know more, I am sharing what I am spiritually aware of now. My purpose is to share the inner worlds, so that readers can awaken in them and know the awe of being more fully human.

Humanity will never be "saved" by a leader, no matter how great. Humanity will come to greatness through every individual becoming a leader in their own life, while still cooperating with their community and allowing, or even enabling, others to play their role. I unashamedly promote this view through all of my books.

The common theme of all my writing is the potential for us all to be spiritual creators with everyone able to participate in their own way. Spiritual warfare happens easily, through confusion and fear as much as by intent. What we collectively need to do now is to learn spiritual cooperation. A step towards this, is an understanding of what is happening in spiritual realms, so that we can respond with wisdom and compassion.

Jack Schouten 1996

GLOSSARY

I have used words that are already in existence but their meanings in this book are frequently different or broader than would be found in any dictionary. This is the case with any vocabulary for a specialized field of knowledge until everyone in that field comes to agreement about their own technical language. At present, while their may be many essential agreements about spiritual realities, there are still many different perspectives and words have been borrowed from different cultures or spiritual streams.

When I borrow words or systems of ideas from existing spiritual movements, it is to enable readers to use their familiarity of existing terms, rather than to recommend any spiritual stream. They can all be of value and it is up to the individual to choose for themselves.

This glossary appears at the front of the book because it could be helpful for some readers, to browse through it before reading the articles.

ACCEPTANCE: To allow ourselves to be affected or organized by what we receive from people or through events.

AFFIRMATIONS: Repetitions of statements that positively establish our self image, attitudes, goals or parameters. These replace, transcend, overcome or resist the forces we have created in the past or which have been accepted from other people's spirits. The empowerment by repetition accumulates so that it is effectively the same or more powerful than an intense emotional involvement or response. Affirmations are taken deeply into ourselves as well as becoming a part of the forces we impose on other people, in an attempt to gain their agreement. The statements are of what we want or believe to be now.

AGENDAS: An essential pattern of goals which we use to organize ourselves and those people we are connected to. Agendas are one of the tools we use to create our future as we wish it. They set clear intuitive patterns for everyone to follow.

ALIGNMENTS: The bringing to harmony of our physical and conditioned body or of our conditioned and desire body as a means of coming to harmony within ourselves or with our group or leader. There can be permanent alignments through initiations where people's bodies are altered to suit the new group or role.

ANGEL: As humans are people oriented most of the positive spiritual forces we perceive are the spiritual presences or effects of other people. They may attempt to guide, guard, goad or god us consciously or intuitively and as a result we can often sense their effects and elucidate their image. Sometimes we may discover ourselves spiritually involved with other people guiding them. We can also perceive forces of the place we are in, of nature, and of the group of people we are a part of, as we spiritually effect each other intuitively.

ARCHETYPES: In seeking with empowered desires we can connect to patterns of possibilities that are available in the groupmind. These are the spiritual essences of prototypal experiences or solutions of individuals or communities who have dealt with situations that have a correspondence to our own imbalance of the moment. The attributes can be evoked and become available and be expressed in a personalized way. These can appear in our imagination or our dreams or in any of our creative expressions in response to us dwelling on an area of imbalance in our lives.

ASPECTS: Distinct areas or qualities of our beings and of the collective. By operating from different aspects of ourselves or by focusing on different aspects of life we evoke different interactions between ourselves and the world.

ASTRAL: a realm of shared imagination where possibilities can be created and explored in a way that can flow through to the physical world. Through our own desires, imaginings and dreams we all participate in the co-operative creation and unfolding of the events of our lives long before they come about. While our astral activities can relate to the physical world, even directly, they can also explore concepts, images, and memories. Our astral activities are continuous whether we are conscious of them or not, until all our desires have been completed or let go. Once we are aware of what is possible we can act in astral realms in a more purposeful way.

ASTRAL BODY: A spiritual aspect of every being which is involved in exploring, preparing, interacting with, creating or unfolding possibilities and events through astral realms. Also called our desire body due to its attempts to bring our desires to completion.

ASTRALITY: The life-energy we dedicate to emotions and desires and our abilities to create, which flows from them.

ASTRAL TRAVEL: The movement of our attention through astral realms. We can carry an image of ourselves and move as we would in the physical world or we can choose places or sites of attention to connect to directly and immediately. When astrally present at a distance we can observe all that we could physically as well and interact with the spiritual aspects of people while there. If we are clairvoyantly focused on while present elsewhere astrally, our image or qualities can be elucidated. We all astral travel every day but we are only conscious of it sometimes.

ATTENTION: The energetic connecting up of our minds with an object, whether it is a physical one or a concept, symbol, image, person or memory. Our attention enables a flow to occur where we can receive from what we focus on or impose ourselves on it, or both. Where our attention has been empowered it is possible for us to continue the flow until it is complete and balance our relationship with what we focus on. Where our minds are attempting to impose on other people's there can be resistance, transformation or transcendence rather than acceptance or expression. As a result we may be altered to suit them rather than the other way around. We intuitively bring our attention to what we appreciate and away from what we dislike.

ATTUNEMENTS: Of our chakras where their function or frequency is altered to create harmony. The attunement can be between the chakras relieving internal personal conflicts and enabling physical health, or between us and others enabling intuitive co-operation to occur more easily.

BARRIERS TO CONSCIOUSNESS: The world is too big for any of us to be aware of completely. We prefer to focus our attention on one or a few areas at a time so that we are not overwhelmed. Our barriers are a form of protection from distraction. There are barriers to our own unconscious material as well as barriers to the minds of other people.

BARRIERS TO TRESPASS: We can selectively open up to other people so that there can be a flow of influence and power between us. If our barriers were not present then we could be psychically available to be changed or robbed by anyone at any time. People who are weakened through trauma or illness often have their barrier selection mechanism too open. Much of life's interplays are about persuading other people to open up or merge with us. People who are too open may be paranoid about being abused. People we trust or members of our groupsoul have a higher level of direct intuitive access to us than others. These barriers are called doorways.

BODY: An interconnected organic whole made up of a collection of aspects of the one kind. Our physical body is the total of our physical aspects, our etheric body the total of our conditioned or trained aspects, our astral body of our desires and aversions. Our ego is the director of these bodies and our self is a combination of our ego with our connections to our community.

BROADCASTING: Every thought, desire or emotion we have can be sent out from us to other people. Anyone who is focused on us, our space or who shares an area of interest with us has the opportunity to perceive whatever we make available whether they bring it to consciousness or not. In times of emotional intensity or distress we broadcast much more powerfully. People who consider something very important or who are very competitive increase their level of intensity of broadcast, in order to get their way.

CALLING TELEPATHICALLY: When we intensely focus our minds on another person we telepathically direct their attention to us. This can be completely intuitive and the person can cooperate with us without being aware that they are doing so. They may remember feeling distracted or being absent minded for a while, doing something unexpected or even remember thoughts that related to us or what we were involved in. This is a normal relationship between children and mothers or pupils and teachers and can also exist between any people who have a connection, even if slight.

CHAKRAS: are sites of connections between our different bodies. There are flows of energy and influence through our chakras organizing relationships within our physical body, between our etheric and other bodies and between ourselves, other people and the world. They have a dynamic relationship with our hormonal systems, affecting them or being affected by them. They can be the doorways to spiritual consciousness or spiritual activities. By directing our attention to our etheric body, we can feel the activity in our chakras. If we have the wisdom to do so safely, we can make changes to many areas of our lives directly through our chakras.

CHANNELS: are like relay stations for radios. They are people who are able to allow other spirits to speak or act through them directly. They can be bridges from the unconscious of their client to consciousness or from other people who wish to speak to their client. They can also channel on their own behalf. Channels differ from mediums in that they have no consciousness of what they are doing at the time.

CHI: A Chinese word for life-energy.

CLAIRAUDIENCE: Something like talking on the phone. It comes to consciousness along our mental pathway of hearing. It can be very valuable but it can also lead to confusion as it is not always possible to know who we are communicating with or whether what we are receiving is of any value. It is possible to learn to recognize people's voices or to feel them out as to the kind of people they are but it helps us if we can also develop our spiritual sight. We can listen to people's minds from a distance, evoke unconscious responses or hear people who are astrally present speaking to us.

CLAIRSENTIENT: There are many spiritual senses including the correlations of physical senses. The physical senses are a pathway to conscious awareness for us and are well developed so that spiritual senses can use their pathways to come to consciousness. We can touch, taste and smell from a distance or sense the astral presence of people with us with these senses as well.

CLAIRVOYANT: Like clairaudient but using the sense of sight. We are usually more subtle visually both in recognition and in the creation or expression of images. The word is often applied to the whole range of personally directed perception with our minds. It is possible to use all of our spiritual senses at once so that we are able to have a fuller communication with others and an experience as if we are completely there with whatever we are focused on..

COMPLETION.: When we are off balance or in need of any kind we create or empower karmic forces in an attempt to restore balance or fulfil the need. Sometimes habits, beliefs, routines, obligations or roles prevent us from allowing the completion of our other forces so that the karmic forces are frustrated and will flow elsewhere.

COMPLETION occurs when we allow the forces to return to harmony. When this applies to relationships with people we will find that all obsessiveness has gone, we can still choose to respond to anyone, but are no longer forced to.

CONDITIONING BODY: The regulator of our automatically limiting, formative or directing forces that ensure that the forces of our desire body, which attempt to expand and create new possibilities, are kept under control. It consists of the sum of all of our previous choices or acceptances taken deeply into ourselves and is our protection from new desire forces. It is also the regulator of all of our physical bodily activities, from behaviour in the world down to our chemical changes. It is the pattern for all our processes. It is a storehouse of life-energy. It is also called our etheric body and it is connected to everyone and everything we have responded to and remain connected to. The formative power of our conditioned body can be loosened up or rearranged so that we can be freed from many of the forces of our past and act in consciousness each moment, or be subjected to a new set of conditioning.

CONNECTION: An ability to merge or share with who or whatever we have focused on. It can be temporary or become habitual so that they continue until altered or completed.

CONSCIOUSNESS: An active giving of attention enabling us to interact with whatever we focus on and bring it into the forum of our mind. Our consciousness depends on what we are able to focus on, how broadly we are able to be focused with energy, or how much of the world we can take in or be ready to interact with. Our consciousness is limited by how much life-energy we dedicate to our attention.

CONVERSION: The letting go of the old and adoption or creation of the new. Personal conversions can relate to a single item or could be a complete brainwashing and re-indoctrination process involving all beliefs, values and goals. Religious conversions enabled people to adapt themselves to the new social world and come to harmony with their new community.

CORRESPONDENCE: Sharing of a natural resonance in essential qualities. A change in one creates a force to create a change in the other which can be felt in the other. From the simple event of items resonating to a common sound to the relationship that the movement of the planets through the zodiac has to all events on earth. As above so below. Both events, even at a distance and of a different nature, can be responses to the same cause so that one event can create a myriad of changes elsewhere.

DESIRES: forces of attraction and creation that lead us to new possibilities of experience. The basis of all change and one of the main causes of conflict.

DESIRE BODY: An other word for astral body. It can consist of the totality of all the incomplete desires we have ever accepted or created. It includes all the propensities, desires and aversions that we brought with us at birth as well as that we have created since. These will continue to be active forces attempting to bring about events until they are completed or disempowered.

DETACHMENT: An ability to personally choose our level and nature of involvement in any event or person. A cessation of merging or flow with all that we are connected to on a habitual level so that we can choose if and how we will be affected or affect others.

DOORWAYS: Avenues for our attention to enter other realms. These can be in or associated with our physical or etheric bodies or can use physical openings symbolically to evoke the same state.

DREAMS: glimpses of the spiritual interplays between levels of ourselves or between ourselves and other people. Can be of the attempts at training our intuitive aspects, reconciling conflicts between new choices and old ones, the exploring or resolution of conflicts between ourselves and other people or aspects of our world, the preparation of future events or spiritual explorations. In our dreams we can be passive observers or we can come to be conscious participants both in our own and other people's dreams. Dreams can be opportunities for other people to spiritually advise or direct our responses to events. Our behaviour in dreams when still unconscious is a combination of how we would habitually respond, what we want to have and how other people expect us to be involved. To some extent all the participants of a dream will experience the same events in their own way with only some ingredients being identical.

EGO: Our "I", That part that is unique to us, the maker of choices and the director of changes to our desire and conditioning body and of all that we give our attention to or actively participate in. It is the enabler of interest and discernment and of the protection from uncertain or unfavourable change. It prevents us from merging with our group totally and organizes and directs what merging we do. If our Ego over protects us from influence it can prevent us benefiting from the communal interplays and reduce our interflow with life. Balancing our ego includes learning to use discernment in what we open to from our groupsoul or groupmind and what we allow ourselves to be changed by.

EGOLESSNESS: Where a person accepts everything from others without reference to their own needs. This is a normal social mechanism in times of trauma where individuals set aside personal forces to be able to cooperate intuitively to collectively deal with the challenge. For some people it becomes a permanent state.

EGOTISM: Where we allow our needs of the moment, whether physical, conditioned or desired, to dictate our involvement with other people or the creation of events. With the development of our "self" comes the possibility of considering both our needs and the needs of our communities.

EMPOWER: To direct a flow of life-energy from or through our selves to the person or objective being supported.

Empowering other people or events enables their completion at which time they can in turn support others. The life-energy flows through a community and is not used up although it can be stored, dissipated or blocked so that the flow appears to dry up. To empower someone else requires us to create a surplus in ourselves first so that when focused on them the flow is to them rather than to us. This empowerment is a key ingredient of spiritual healing.

ENERGY: That which is needed to go from one form or state to another. That which is absorbed or released when a change of form occurs. While physical energy relates to physical effects life-energy is held in conditioning or life forms and patterns. We can give out this energy to other people as grace, metta, love, prana, chi etc or we can use it to empower our visualizations or agendas creating forms for the future.

ENERGY BODIES: Our spiritual forms that in their patterning hold life-energy. Each persons energy body is constantly changing according to the interplay of life. Rebuilding itself with every new choice or option accepted. They hold the total of all limiting forces we impose on the world or on our own physical body. Another name for our formative, etheric or conditioned body.

ENERGY CONVERSIONS: Where old patterns, forms and desires are let go of to make the energy available again for other purposes. In everyday relaxation some energy conversion occurs, in kundalini it occurs in a far more powerful and rapid way. There are many energy conversion techniques for people to provide the life-energy they need.

ETHERIC: relates to our life-energy and to our conditioning body as well as the patterns behind all of life and its myriad expressions. It is also a form of resonance tying together beings of the one kind or purpose.

ETHERIC BODY: Our conditioned body which is also a coordinator of the interactions between our physical body, our desire body, our community and our spirit. Our pattern or etheric body is present while alive and when we enliven it with our energy it is able to restore our physical body to its ideal state. The patterns remain but other demands temporarily pull our physical body out of alignment with them. Meditating on our physical body can lead to the restoration of health by enabling the alignment between bodies to occur.

ETHERIC FLOWS: The flow of energy and influence along habitual pathways. Flows within an individual, between individuals, through a group, in every living being and over the earth itself. The flows can be altered or rearranged by a direction of consciousness.

ETHERIC PROJECTION: A correspondence or summary of a person which can interact with events at a distance as their go between. Being identical with the essence of the person and intimately connected with them it is as if the person and their consciousness is actually present. These are considered to be ghosts when seen but are usually aspects of living people. The etheric projection can be completely independent of a physical body or only partially connected so that an etheric nose, arm or leg is able to operate independently and act according to our will and interact with people and objects at a distance. Just as we can have our attention in our etheric body while in place with our physical body we can maintain our attention in it while it is away and in a sense our being is away with it. The nature of resonating patterns is such that part of a pattern can be identical to the whole so that while we may feel a loss of life-energy we do not lose the original pattern itself when the projection is independent from our physical bodies.

EVENT: On a simple level it is the point in time and space at which there is a possibility for us to get what we want, and there is a transfer of some kind, whether of goods, experience, influence or life-energy between people which results in a change in them. Events have several sets of forces active in them with all the routine predictable ingredients as the warp of the tapestry with the new, incomplete or even unpredictable ingredients as the weft. Each person brings to an event something different and receives from it in a personal way. The event is the culmination, incarnation and expression of a set of interrelated spiritual forces which may have been in preparation for years. In turn, events are the beginnings of new forces which can continue to have an influence rippling out for centuries.

FEARS: A fleeing within ourselves from a fixation on a negative possibility. Confidence is an assumption of positive harmonious consequences and events. Confident people see misfortunes as aberrations to their lives that can be disregarded, fearful people see them as normal and accept them as their patterns for creating the future. A withdrawal of our life-energy occurs when we are fearful as we battle for control over negativity's rather than letting them go and assuming, empowering and enabling positive possibilities instead.

FORCES: The potentials and tendencies for the creation of a change. Personal forces include All of our desires and habits.

FOUNDATIONS: Essential patterns that we have created or accepted for ourselves from goals and parameters. These become our reference points with which to explore new possibilities.

GODS: collective forces. Could describe the all or the totality of all there is, the spiritual influence of a community or society or be individual forces that people perceive as originating outside themselves. Some people regard their spiritual guides or guardians as gods because of their apparent superhuman abilities.

GRACE: A Christian name for life-energy, pure support or love.

GROUP: consisting of people who share something in common, so that their attention is able to link up at times.

GROUPSOUL: The arena for intuitive interactions between people who have accepted connections with or through each other, usually as a result of historical relationships. Our groupsoul is our inner circle of support and intuitive influence. The people may not have met but need to be acceptable to each other. Each person's groupsoul is slightly different.

GROUPMIND: consists of aspects of the minds of people who have focused on common areas of interest rather than on each other as individuals. These people may intuitively or consciously share the same subject of interest with each other without having met at all.

GROUPSPIRIT: The essence that enables the group to have the identity and spiritual influence that it does.

GUIDANCE: Suggestions given or received with the idea of influencing a persons direction in life.

HEALING: The enabling of a positive change at any level of our being.

IMAGINATION: A world between our minds and souls and the souls of everyone else, and between possibility and the current material reality, in which we can create or explore, draw from or be guided through. It can relate to the physical world, whether directly or through symbols or metaphors, or to pure thought, independent of material reality. It is fluid and able to be affected by physical experiences as well as able to affect them. In participating, in realms of the imagination we contribute to the creation of forces that can flow through to future physical events if they find agreement. Somewhere between inspiration and intuition.

IMPULSES: Forces pushing us to react, act or speak. More powerful than suggestions, which are options to explore.

INCARNATION: The expression of spiritual forces in the physical world. These forces may have been in preparation for centuries and may be blended from a range of different sources. People incarnate as well as events co-operatively created by them.

INNER WORLDS: that which we experience as separate from our physical reality. It can be of our own creating or cosmic reality, experienced alone or with our groupsouls or groupminds.

INDIVIDUAL: Separate and distinct. Each of us has aspects which we share with our groups and aspects we have made for ourselves which we may hold onto despite the conflict they cause with our groups. An individual has assessed their qualities and chosen, felt out or adapted them themselves whether they are identical with other people's or unique. An individual in themselves is the source of the forces they impose on the world.

INITIATES: People who have come to selfhood and who are able to co-ordinate community events through spiritual realms. There are unconscious initiates who are not aware of their spiritual activities but who have developed them far enough to be able to create and co-ordinate changes at a community level by their balanced thinking, feeling and willing. Conscious initiates would essentially act in the same way spiritually but have some awareness of what they are involved in and can make adjustments as they go if necessary. According to their different levels of ability initiates can co-ordinate a skill or a profession or guide communities or nations, working with or through the people without needing to be present physically.

INITIATION: A process usually under the direction of teachers or elders enabling a person to undergo a rapid change into an alignment with a new group or as a preparation for a new role or stage of life. During the initiation process many of a persons personal patterns are broken or disempowered, putting a person in a position where they can adopt a series of new patterns easily, either from their new group or by choosing a new set themselves. When the initiation is into a group, the whole process may be over in hours or days with little consciousness of the change on the part of the individuals involved. Where the individual goes through the process alone they may take years to do so in which case the initiation is to selfhood.

INSPIRATION: Allowing a spiritual influence, or material from the groupmind, to enter into us and come to consciousness. We can focus our attention by asking a question precisely and then allowing the response to return to us or we can open up to what naturally resonates and comes to us.

INTUITION: Something we perceive from unconscious aspects of ourselves or beyond that we become aware of through our body, actions or words rather than in full consciousness. Intuition is more of a feeling out of the world and of our response to it than a process of thought as in inspiration.

KARMA: We arrive at birth with a range of personal forces which motivate and limit us and participate in the creation of all the events of our lives. At every moment, with every experience, thought, feeling or desire, aversion or fear, we are completing or altering our karmas. We can create and empower any future we choose for ourselves and if it is acceptable to our communities or if we are single-minded and powerful enough it will come about. The development of our karma is a dynamic affair with everyone we interact with contributing to it. Many of the forces we hold and empower are shared with other people so that there can be personal karmas, family karmas, national karmas and karmas of an age. By always choosing the positive and valuable for ourselves in harmony with our community, we create a good karma from which positive events in life will flow.

KUNDALINI: a process of rapid energy conversion moving energy between the chakras and spiritual bodies. Kundalini can be a natural process of energy redistribution which can be brought under conscious direction. While it can be induced it is not advisable unless our energies are already in balance as any imbalance will be highlighted or expressed to be dealt with after an intense energy flow.

LIFE-ENERGY: the vital forces enabling the creation of forms and changes to them. Life-energy can be felt and experienced on an etheric level without being detected in any physical way until it creates a change there. It can be experienced within ourselves as a flow of changes in our body and felt flowing between us and other people who are physically present or at a distance. In relaxation we bring it to balance and in contraction we draw it in or send it out. With our attention, particularly in meditation, we can move it around within ourselves or between ourselves and other people or to future events. When used in healing it can be felt as a flow of warmth as it enables a flow and relaxation to occur.

LIFE FORCE: The flavour of life energy or the influence it has.

LIFE FORCE ENERGY: Both empowerment and influence.

MEDITATION: Choosing to direct our mind in consciousness. We can in meditation direct our attention to our bodies, our breath, visualizations of role models or our desires, concepts and subjects of interest, imagination and invention, intuition, nature, into other realms, or more mindfully into the tasks we are engaged in or allow ourselves to come to stillness. Meditation is an act of assertiveness where we choose to enable our own interests, personal forces or health needs, direct our creative processes, or choose to open up to new perceptions.

MEDIUMS: Mediums bring to their consciousness some of the spiritual forces available from other people or their guides. Unlike channels they can use their discernment to choose what to share with their clients and to present it to them in their own way. They differ from clairvoyants in that while conscious of what comes to mind they are not conscious of where it comes from. Mediums may have clairvoyant people as their spiritual guides, astrally present with them to assist them. Anyone who is connected to them, or their client, can also provide information to them spiritually.

MERIDIANS: Pathways of life-energy flows in our

etheric bodies. When we bring our attention to this body, ours or someone else's, we can feel the flow of energy as well as the shortages and congestions. The continual balanced flow of life-energy enables us to keep ourselves in harmony and health.

METTA: A buddhist word for life-energy. We are able to accumulate it in ourselves or make available to others.

MIND: The arena of our possible consciousness where our spirit can work to make changes to aspects of our souls, our desires or patterns, or our activities in the physical world. In the active sense our mind is the vehicle for our spirits or other people's through which changes are made within ourselves and in the world. While there can be interactions or even battles between minds it is actually the spirit's forces working through them which are active. In our minds we can bring together our perceptions from different realms to explore them and compare them with other experiences

OBJECTS OF ATTENTION: Anything that we can live in for a while with our attention. The result of a connection with them is an experience through our minds that corresponds to what is available at our point of focus. We can be focused on ideas, images or memories among many possibilities.

OPENNESS: Allowing in spiritual forces. People can become neurotic, compulsive or gullible in extreme cases of openness, or psychotic when open but acting in reaction to what is received. With discernment openness is the basis of effective intuitive cooperation. If openness develops in proportion to self knowledge and awareness it is awe inspiring in what we can have access to.

OPENING UP: A changing of gears, states of mind or redirection of attention. It is also the alteration or activation of chakras to allow perception of spiritual realms or the entry of spiritual forces. In many ways a temporary merging between ourselves and whatever we seek out or is available from our community or cosmos. Opening up can be conscious, a result of our desires or habits or accidental. We can seek a doorway out and an attitude to go with or we can focus on a destination allowing our spiritual journey to occur intuitively.

PERCEPTION: An ability to connect our attention with possible points of experience so that we can receive something from them.

POSSESSION: Where the forces received from our unconscious, the minds of other people or the building we are in, are accepted completely rather than explored as options. A possessed individual has lost the ability to discern or choose for themselves as a result of an imbalance. It is usually temporary but with some people may be permanent where they are organized by their community completely. Can occur for the duration of a trauma or a war as a means of protecting an individual from being integrally affected by experiences that are overwhelming them, and enables co-operative activities to be co-ordinated easily by those people who remain confident and disciplined. Where the possession is at a group level it is the identity or the spirit of the group that is holding them through their collective patterning.

PRANA: A Hindu word for life-energy.

PRAYER: The direction of our mind into or through spiritual realms for a purpose of influence or support, for ourselves or others. While the intention is usually conscious the process of bringing about results spiritually may not be. Prayer can be direct to the object of desire, to the possible people involved or through a "divine" intermediary.

REALMS: Distinct areas that our attention can go to, the physical world and our memory as well as spiritual worlds associated with the physical world, images and concepts. They contain the past and preparations for the future.

RECEPTIVE: Where our attention is not engaged elsewhere and we are in a mode of appreciation. In this state influences can come to us from our personal unconscious or other people and nature, without our ego reacting to it.

RELIGIOUS CONVERSIONS: Processes of letting go

and rebuilding where the indoctrination is for. a religious agenda or into a religious group.

RESONANCE: An ability to accept a flow of influence or energy due to a correspondence in essential nature between an aspect of ourselves and of something else. Resonance enables us to be affected by the stars or by minute doses of homeopathic medicine. Our essences have a natural connection to all that we can resonate with. There can be resonance between qualities, ideas, and objects that we can intuitively feel out.

REPRESSION: the creation of forces which we do not allow to be consciously expressed so that they go through other realms or await a future opportunity.

RITUAL: A series of defined activities that have been habitually imbued with meaning that enable the participants to alter or establish their relationships with each other or the world in a harmonious way.

SELF: or Higher Self. We have the physical body, the conditioned body, the desire body, the ego and the self. The self comes into being naturally as we develop and bring to balance our other bodies and our relationship with our community and cosmos. Our "self" is something we usually need to find and it is brought to fulfilment through life's experiences. When we act from our ego we are maintaining a separateness from our community for protection, when we act from our selves we allow our beings to have access to our unconscious and to merge with our community knowing that through self knowledge we are whole and will not be adversely affected. In acting from our selves we intuitively coordinate or direct many of our communities activities as well, as our interests in many areas are shared.

Our "self" is sometimes categorized into a higher self, a self meaning our "I" or ego, and our physical, conditioned and desire bodies called our lower self. There is a truth in this as our self contains them all. We can interact with the world from any spiritual body and in each person a different one can be temporarily dominant. In harmony we can consider all of our bodies at once.

SELFHOOD.: Completion of our selves.

SOUL: The feeling part of ourselves that can interact with life in a personal way and express the group forces in an individual way. Our soul includes both our desire body and our conditioned body and how much "soul" we have depends on how much we have unfolded or enlivened these and made them our own or found our own being in them. A troubled soul can result from a conflict between these two aspects or a conflict between our soul and our groupsoul. Loss of soul can happen as a result of any trauma or long term deprivation and is only a temporary state. Our soul becomes active again when our confidence and comfort in our own being returns.

SOUL PUPIL: someone who is learning from a guide through their astral or intuitive connections.

SPIRIT: Our essential being which works through our other bodies to guide our activities in all realms. In turn it is developed by the accumulation of all essential experiences we go through. Through an expansion of consciousness our spirit can grow and become the master of other bodies. It can act independently of our conditioning or desires or community expectations and can flavor all that we are involved in. Our spirit is our I but perceived in its entirety. While our spirit is the essence of all that we have chosen in our lives, all that we experience is also an expression of our spirit.

SPIRITUAL: While it could refer to the essential totality of who we are, with our physical aspects being the expressed part of it in the material realm, it is often used to refer to the non physical aspects of life. Sometimes people who are not focused on material aspects of life are called spiritual indicating where their attention, or their foundations for life, usually are.

SPIRITUAL ASSISTANTS: People who assist through spiritual means. This could be through their astral presence exploring situations or guiding people or telepathically responding to our requests with suggestions. We all intuitively assist each other through spiritual realms so to some extent we are all spiritual assistants. Some people bring the process to consciousness so that they can assist others more appropriately or make greater use of the spiritual assistance available.

SPIRITUAL GUIDES: Spiritual assistants who take the initiative in choosing or creating new possibilities for those they spiritually work with. They can be conscious of their spiritual activity or their guidance can flow naturally out of their everyday relationships and abilities.

SPIRITUAL HEALING: the bringing of an aspect of another person to balance or completion through what flows spiritually from or through the healer. A sharing of life-energy can occur to enable a person to heal themselves or where a person is of the same groupsoul and they are in conflict, their etheric patterning can be affected to bring them into alignment with the group and themselves. All spiritual healing, other than the giving of life-energy or the unblocking of a persons own flows, are forms of dominance where the person healing is able to make available healthy patterns that replace existing negative ones. Health is normal when we are in harmony within ourselves and with our group unless we have exhausted our life-energy. Where we ensure we have a surplus of energy our beings will automatically bring us back to harmony at all levels.

SPIRITUAL REALMS: In this book usually refers to any of the non material realms.

SPIRITUAL PROTECTION: The shielding from inappropriate influence or trespass through spiritual realms. This could be created by being only selectively open ourselves or could be through our group where our guides select what we can become involved in. It is possible to use symbols and rituals to evoke different levels of openness or closedness in ourselves or the protection can result from an ego activity. In knowing ourselves we can be less easily affected by what we receive.

SPIRITUAL WARFARE: Can be similar to spiritual healing in many ways except that the process is reversed. Life-energy may be drained and conflicts created to unbalance the person. Most spiritual warfare is unintentional and can occur between two people of goodwill if their unconscious differences are too great. All conflict can be sorted out if the people have enough surplus life-energy to give to it. The process of expanding ourselves to come to terms with a range of people and positions, creates a foundation from which we are better able to deal with conflict at any level in the future.

SUPERSENSIBLE: Beyond our physical senses but available to our spiritual senses.

SUPRACONSCIOUSNESS: A pool of resources spiritually available to us which is beyond our own personal resources and is able to extend to include all beings. Through our connections with other people there is a possibility for them to intuitively share all that they wish to broadcast.

TELEPATHY: A process of sharing with people with our minds. This can be two ways through being focused on each other but often it is a matter of one person allowing in or accepting the distress calls of someone who may not realize they are broadcasting powerfully. Usually the receiving of words, concepts or images but can also be complete detailed experiences from physical or spiritual realms.

TRANSCENDANCE: The expansion of our spiritual being so that we are able to incorporate the essence of new forces. In this way we can come to harmony with other people who may have different parameters and goals to us. Most understanding of new material occurs through transcendence. It is distinctly different from acceptance in that it includes the process of reconciliation with our existing material or positions.

TRANSFORMATION: An alteration of inappropriate or unwanted influences to acceptable ones. Where trancendence enables harmony between people and positions transformation simply replaces one set with another. The process can occur at a completely intuitive level where the dominant members of a group replace all unwanted influences without considering how it will affect other people. When an influence is received it can be reformed and rebroadcast to suit their own agendas where in turn it may be transformed by someone else. In self transformation we replace unwanted agendas and parameters with newly chosen ones.

TRANSITIONS: a passage from one state to another. Personal transitions include all of our life changes and the changes in the groups, partners, jobs, houses, towns we are a part of.

TRANSPERSONAL: Realms of the intuitive sharing between people that we can learn to direct our conscious attention to.

TRAUMA: A severe frustration to the expected flow of life. Usually requires a process of reorientation as part of the healing as there is an involuntary letting go of old dreams, self image or beliefs. The inner process of reconciliation and rebuilding draws all of a person's attention and life-energy inwards so that little is available for conscious physical life.

UNCONSCIOUS: Beyond the reach of ordinary consciousness. Much of our personal unconscious originated through our conscious activities but was rejected or denied further access to consciousness. As a result unconscious forces must find other means to be completed. Our unconscious has habitual bridges through other realms and our forces can affect other people. Our unconscious contents also include all that we were born with or have received intuitively that has yet to come to consciousness.

VISUALIZATIONS: The bringing of selected material to mind imaginatively from where it can be taken more deeply into ourselves, altered or broadcast into our community. We can visualize the image of a saint or qualities we wish to emulate or we can prepare an image to send to someone, or we can create the patterns for a future event we have an interest in. Visualizations are shared so that they can be received from other people particularly if they are given prompts to tune into. A visualization can be completely fluid and held amongst a group of minds with each person contributing. In the process of visualizing we connect up to their contents so that they can be affected and either change our relationship to them or alter future events.

CHAPTER ONE

OUR NATURAL

SPIRITUAL

ACTIVITIES

Our personal spiritual potential is enormous, whether we have discovered it yet or not. Instead of trying to train our spiritual abilities we can bring the natural processes, that we have always been a part of, to consciousness. With understanding we can learn to use them in a more purposeful or directed way.

I. *Implications of spiritual awareness*

Whether we are conscious of it or not, we are constantly communicating with each other with our minds or with aspects of our spiritual beings. There is a constant flow of thoughts and images, desires, feelings and impulses, flowing naturally along habitual pathways between people who are connected.

The flow between us can also be shared precisely by focusing our attention on someone, or something they are connected to, or we can broadcast indiscriminately to anyone who is receptive.

After coming to stillness we can consciously perceive what is available to us from others or we can direct our attention with precision to any place, time, person, concept or image to observe what is available there or to spiritually interact with it.

Most people have had intuitions, hunches or premonitions, out of body experiences or been temporarily telepathic or have noticed their desires coming true at times with little effort. As a result we all know that there are other levels to life and that these experiences are glimpses of what is going on continually, without us being conscious of them. Some people purposefully set about to find their way through barriers to consciousness in these realms or prepare themselves to open up to awaken in them.

All that occurs in our minds can intuitively flow out to anything in the world that relates to it. Similarly expressions from other minds flow into ours. Much that is new that occurs in our minds comes from elsewhere.

As we are human and often focused on people what we receive is usually from other people, who may have no idea that they are sharing with us. It could be drawn from their conscious thoughts and desires or be intuitive responses to our questions from their training.

We are all naturally intuitive as a matter of course but much of what is available is screened out from us. However, some still affects us intuitively without us realizing and only a small part of what we could have access to ever comes to consciousness. Telepathy uses the same process as any intuition but with a different level of consciousness. What we send can be at different intensities due to different levels of emotional involvement, and we can be open to different extents due to our state of mind or our relationship to the person sending. At times it helps if the person it is being sent to, and the material being transferred, is fully focused on but often this is not necessary as we may be habitually open to it or the sender.

Everyone intuitively participates in enabling possibilities for each other or attempts to regulate each others beliefs, goals or behaviour. When we understand this we can use our thoughts to provide other people with a smorgasbord of possibilities to choose from, while allowing them their freedom to live as they wish.

People usually spend their lives interconnected with people with similar or complementary agendas and beliefs so that in many areas of our daily life it would not be possible to distinguish the essence of our thoughts and desires from those of someone we are close to. It is often possible to discern the thoughts of strangers before those of our friends, as we can more easily discern the presence of unusual thoughts.

Most people have trained their subconscious to screen out the reception of inappropriate material or impulses that arrives unless it comes from accepted members of their groupsoul or it is relevant to their current interest. If we wish to expand our awareness of inner worlds we need to thin out or push some of these subconscious barriers back a little. Alternatively we can find a way to temporarily set the barriers aside.

The forces that flow to us from others interact with the existing forms that we have created by choosing or accepting. In areas in which we have strong foundations we will be unaffected or transform the forces we receive intuitively to suit ourselves. When we are fully focused on our own agendas and live within our own parameters what we receive spiritually will have little chance to be expressed through us. However if we are uncertain or incomplete we may have room to accommodate new material, possibilities or influences.

When receptive we might intuitively respond by phoning or visiting people or knowing what to do, when to do it or what questions to ask. We may even discover that we have been influenced to the point of letting go of major goals or beliefs and adopting new ones without being conscious of the process of change. This intuitive process enables a community to constantly stay in tune as the cultural influences change.

While mediums and clairvoyants may consciously tune into unconscious aspects of their clients, to a lesser extent doctors and healers can often intuitively diagnose illnesses, counsellors intuitively ask the right questions and businessmen follow hunches about possible courses of action, without questioning how. If we observe our everyday conversations and notice anything that is unexpected we could ask what is organizing it. If we focus our thoughts and resist an impulse or desire to speak, often someone else will raise the subject for us or answer it or be affected by the contents of our thoughts.

We radiate the essence of what we are, want, believe, know or create constantly into the transpersonal realms in an attempt to make the world into our own chosen image. We are particularly powerful in this in times that our thoughts and desires are clear and directed. By changing ourselves and the contents of our thoughts and desires we change the effect we have on the world.

As we share influence we also share life-energy with

anyone we support in order to enable ourselves and others to complete the karmic forces, which we all have created to fulfil our needs. We can use our personal power to impose on others or to give the surplus away generously to contribute to the unfolding of our community.

Whenever we have an attitude that something is of great importance or urgency our single-mindedness ensures that all our available energy and support goes into it. People we are connected to will intuitively respond and assist us astrally or physically in times of need or trauma, giving or doing what they can to help.

There are people who have enormous missions in life, to create a business empire, political influence, or spiritual stream, which could affect a whole nation. They may need many people to contribute and influence many individuals to organize their lives to suit the mission. The leader, using both physical means and their minds, will be broadcasting their agendas for change, with many associates and followers acting as channels and relay stations for their will.

Intuitive sharing between people can continue in a random way or some of the individuals can become conscious of the process and be more purposeful in their thoughts.

Many people are naturally conscious of their spiritual activities and in addition many people train themselves to become so. As a result some people can consciously guide or direct others or a group of awakened people can share astrally or telepathically as they wish.

Some people are able to develop the breadth of their attention to be available to act consciously in spiritual realms while going about their daily lives as easily as other people can drive their car while having a phone conversation. Others may act intuitively at all times without any awareness of what they are involved in but through their natural goodwill have a positive effect on their community. People who are sometimes awake in spiritual realms will still have a continuing intuitive interflow as well between them and others, according to the established foundations, life patterns and agendas of the individuals involved.

As a civilisation we are now familiar with the physical world and have come to accept particular concepts of time and space, matter and energy that apply here. While there are spiritual truths, patterns and parameters these are different to physical realm ones. If we set the physical realm scientific laws aside and explore spiritual realms afresh, while still using the tools of analysis and discernment we have learnt, we can find new truths and enable a more valuable relationship with these realms and with spiritual aspects of ourselves.

Coming to know spiritual realms is in many ways similar to exploring a foreign country and culture. It can be exhilarating and exhausting and make us aware of many conflicts or confusions in our life that we will need time to clarify and reconcile. We can dip in and out of these realms in stages, becoming familiar with different levels as we do so. Maintaining our own balance and morality is more important than developing powerful abilities.

The forces we impose on our community were brought with us at birth and added to each moment of our lives. In conscious sharing we can learn to select most of what we send to someone but at first we may simply react instinctively to anything we become conscious of. At other levels during our communication, we will also intuitively share any of our essence as we respond from our conditioning or desires to anything we spiritually perceive.

We can come to observe our minds to choose the best and to limit impositions on other people. Through coming to clarity and balance in ourselves, learning to perceive the spiritual forces at work and considering the needs of everyone we can participate in enabling our community to come to fulfilment and harmony.

Spiritual cooperation requires us to think and create with an awareness of who or what we connect up with or act on spiritually. At times of spiritual awakening it is apparent that we are all connected so that personal benefit is not as relevant as collective unfolding or completion.

What occurs unconsciously between two people considerably affects their relationship in the physical world. If our thoughts and desires towards people are compatible with their own or if they are open to change our forces will be accepted and they will feel positive about us. Some people find themselves very attractive without ever making any effort in a physical sense. It may be the influence of their minds that people find appealing or persuasive.

It is possible to constantly create and empower new desires with agendas, prayers, resolutions, affirmations, or visualizations. There are many books on how to be successful which offer many different techniques. While enabling personal success these may not address or even mention what we are doing spiritually to achieve it. With wisdom about the spiritual processes and clarity in ourselves we can still be successful while also enabling other people.

The human mind is vast in potential and some people have made far greater use of it than others to the point that it may be difficult to believe or understand what is possible for them. People with great powers rarely publicise their abilities because they need to avoid creating conflicts through fear or negativity, and to avoid unnecessary interference or scrutiny in their lives.

Our personal spiritual potential is enormous too, whether we have discovered it yet or not. Instead of trying to train our spiritual abilities we can bring the natural processes, that we have always been a part of, to consciousness. With understanding we can learn to use them in a more purposeful or directed way.

The unfolding of our spiritual consciousness is a natural one that the whole of the cosmos is a party to, we needn't hurry or worry but can make the most of each moment and every event that enables us to awaken further.

2 Spiritual forces of nature and of humanity.

It is possible to feel the flow of energy in rocks and crystals and to sense plants and animals asserting themselves on the world, through their life forces. We can also imaginatively elucidate the purposes or destiny of plants at any part of their life cycle. Their whole being is available at any time, the tree in the seed as a form which will gradually unfold when possible.

Every being contributes in their own way to the interplay of life and can evolve through their involvement in it. Each animal and plant allows cosmic, groupsoul or forces of nature, to flow through them in different ways and will reflect in their being the geography they live in and their relationship with their worlds.

All beings can have an influence on us, if we open up to them, whether they are appear minute or of the stars. Each day of our lives we can note a change in our moods and yearnings that nature or the cosmos evokes in us. These could relate to our movement through the seasons or to the earth's movement through the zodiac. If we are perceptive enough we could know the week of the year from what we could sense within ourselves, feeling the differences in the type of impulse, interest or way of being.

The regular, cyclical changes in nature have been influential in establishing order in human life and they have provided a framework for our cosmo-conceptions and our purpose for life. The cosmic forces are enabling mankind to unfold just as a seed is enabled to become a tree. Our minds have been influenced by cosmic forces just as our bodies have also been shaped by interactions with nature and the physical world.

There are many forces active in our lives. We may see these as positive or negative but the whole range can be involved in supporting the foundations of our beings. All the forces can play a part in human life and if some are denied or ignored it can be to our cost. By coming to understand the different kinds of spiritual forces we can make use of their positive value.

There are many different kinds of forces, having many different names in different cultures. All of them can tantalise us through the power of the experiences they can enable but they can also unbalance us and alienate us from human life, or our humanity, if dwelt on exclusively.

As mankind began to mentally and physically contribute to the forces at work, and gradually began to refine them, we began to take a greater role in the creative process.

Humans created artefacts as an expression of divine forces we felt within ourselves. The cultural artefacts, in turn, created in our communities a state of mind through which we could be uplifted and nurtured further.

We have developed an active collective mind which has evolved with every experience any individual has learnt from. This has been refined further as we learnt to remember our histories and to compare our cultures.

To some extent our history defines who we are as a nation or people, so that if we allow a fixed history we could be held in a particular image or way of relating to the world. Fortunately history is a fluid force which people imaginatively reinterpret daily, altering the collective self image in the process, enabling us to come to terms with the present and to prepare for the future.

Gradually mankind has learnt, and will learn further, to define ourselves as we wish to be. By doing so we can come to create our future as we wish it.

Over time the influences of the collective mind have become more active so that in modern times they appear to be more influential than forces of nature or the cosmos. Even our physical bodies and appearances owe much to collective ideals, being shaped through human spiritual forces more strongly now than through our interactions with nature.

While we can come to determine our own future in many ways, our sphere of influence is confined to that which we can claim as our own. There will always be a dynamic relationship between mankind and the rest of the cosmos.

In moments of uncertainty we can still refer back to the truths inherent in nature, which can continue as our foundations through all of our explorations and changes.

3. Our personally created spiritual forces.

As we live we take into ourselves from our physical and spiritual experiences and make all that we accept or choose our own. All that we take in becomes a part of the forces that we impose on the world. In consciousness we can alter how we are affected and what we impose on other people. We can choose what to be a part of, direct our level of involvement and select how we will be affected by the experience. Later, as details arise in our minds, we can review, further refine and empower the personal forces we are happy with and let go of, or disempower, the rest.

All the decisions we made in the past, all the desires, aversions and inhibitions, can still be at work organizing our lives for us. Each psychic force we empower at any time in our lives is active until it is expressed, completed, transformed, transcended or disempowered by an active process of letting go. The forces can last all our lives and beyond and are part of what are called our karmic forces.

The totality of what we have created, chosen or accepted over a lifetime is enormous, particularly compared to what we are conscious of each moment. To some extent each small part is still active in organizing our lives and our relationships with the world and choosing its moment to come to consciousness.

In reviewing who we are we can bring these forces to consciousness to choose again. If we don't deal with them they will find their points of possibility for expression and events will occur in the physical world in an attempt to bring them to completion or balance. If not completed, when they arise in our thoughts, dreams or events, we may unsuspectingly empower them further, leading to more events in the future.

We know roughly what we believe in but perhaps not why. We know generally what our goals are but can often find ourselves working towards goals that we had forgotten about and at times expressing original reactions that surprise us.

Just as we train our automatic pilots to drive a car, we train ourselves in every area of life. Each process of learning takes in and locks up some energy which can be available to us in the future. Familiar tasks flow easily while new choices can create conflict and sometimes an enormous amount of reconciliation with the old is necessary. Some decisions to change require an almost total reassessment of who we are before we can make them. This process can be very exhausting and bring us to a complete standstill if severe enough so that for self protection it is often avoided.

We can accept all the old forces that we brought with us at birth and added to each day of our life as being our own, or even who we are, or we can choose anew in every area of life, creating for ourselves a completely new set of forces. The forces we create attract a response from other people which can come to us spiritually or organize physical events in our lives. The directed spiritual guidance we receive from other people often results from how the forces we express have been perceived and is a reflection of who we are and of our relationship with the world.

4 *Our unconscious forces and their spiritual activity.*

Our consciousness deals with changes, leaving intact that wealth of material that we have already learnt, accepted or reconciled, to our conditioning body and our goals, desires and aversions to our astral or desire body. These bodies each of us has are far greater than the consciousness of the moment and are growing or altered with each physical or spiritual experience.

It is possible to act completely in the moment, addressing the unique possibilities freshly each time, while referring to other considerations without being bound by them. This takes a level of clarity, time and energy that most of us do not have so that it is normal to develop patterns by which we can respond to situations without needing additional effort or thought. These patterns may be sourced in our beliefs, knowledge, habits and routines or they can be created through empowering our desires and images of how we would like ourselves, or our futures, to be. The patterns we create all contribute to organizing our futures for us.

As we experience, think, feel or desire we are also empowering our conditioning and goals and taking them into ourselves more deeply where they can continue to organize our lives for us unconsciously. Eventually the accumulation of our unconscious forces is such that they usually dominate our lives unless we constantly let the unnecessary forces go and choose to act in consciousness, and continually reinspire ourselves to be able to do so.

Our unconscious forces can at times override our conscious choices and dominate the moment against our intentions. We could describe this as our spirit being dominated by our soul forces or our astral body dominating our EGO or I. In many ways this is our spiritual challenge, to enable our own spirits to become the masters of our beings and our own lives, so that we can cooperate and assert ourselves only when necessary.

This dominance by our unconscious forces can be a form of self protection that assumes that the accumulated wisdom of a lifetime or a community is of more value than the suggestions or possibilities of the moment. The value of our unconscious activities depends on how well we have selected them each moment of our lives or how valuable the source was that we accepted them from.

While the action of our unconscious forces is obvious when we observe our habitual responses or addictions occasionally, they are at work every moment through our spiritual interactions. What we have created for ourselves in all of those short moments of conscious choice or acceptance has accumulated to become the deeper source of all of our events and relationships of the future, unless we change them.

As we receive from the minds of other people we intuitively respond, organizing our involvement in future events and their lives or in actively preventing it. At the same time we are trying to shape who they are and how they will participate in our events. We could be subservient, assertively cooperative or domineering in our interactions with them.

All that we create or receive with our minds continues to flow intuitively between ourselves and those people we share with, particularly when two people are intimately focused on each other. In the exchange there can be a healing as one person resolves the fears or issues of the other or there could be a spreading of negativities if neither person has yet learnt to transcend or transform them. All healers or counsellors are constantly challenged to heal or prepare themselves in new areas lest they be overwhelmed by what they intuitively receive from their clients. A tempting alternative to this approach is to become mechanically detached from those being treated so that no flow can occur or it can be limited to a very narrow area.

Mediums and clairvoyants usually communicate with these unconscious aspects of people, consciously, and can be a bridge to consciousness for them. Their spiritual communication can be specific to their client or to any of the people their client is connected to, to gain broader insights. Through their connections relatives and friends can be called in to contribute. Their contributions are usually from their unconscious or intuitive aspects. In this way the clairvoyant or medium taps into the future that is being planned by the whole groupsoul rather than just the individual consulting them.

Often in life we create, or allow, conflicting tendencies in our desires, feelings, beliefs and inhibitions. Rather than sort them out immediately we could repress the ones we feel aren't appropriate to the moment and prevent them being expressed or coming to consciousness. As we repress we additionally empower the forces behind the contents until something we are no longer conscious of can come to rule our lives and our relationships with other people. In the process of camouflaging our repressed contents much related material is often blocked from consciousness as well.

These repressed, or shadow, forces can be positive as well as negative and can also arise through love or compassion where the actions which could flow out of the feelings are blocked on a physical level because we feel them to be unsuitable to the moment. The forces we repress or empower further will continue ever more subtly and affect other people spiritually as well as being expressed intuitively without our conscious involvement. They will continue to be active through the spiritual realms, without us being conscious of them, until they can be expressed or completed as these are the moments at which we can let them go.

At times we may wish to express our feelings but not be able to because intuitive forces, from ourselves, or other people, prevent it. We may not have sufficient energy at that moment to assert our wishes or impulses and unless we actively let the energy go or transcend it we will take it into ourselves where it will accumulate instead. It is often what we create but do not express or complete which is active astrally.

We may have loved a person from afar for many years but have had inadequate opportunities to express or complete it, so that we always intuitively give them loving support and create something positive in anything associated with them.

By not expressing our feelings or desire forces on purpose or because of fear, they grow more powerful. Repressing negative feelings and impulses can create powerful negative forces that can contribute to misfortune and diminish everyone they connect with.

By repressing or continually re-empowering our positive forces we create a positive spiritual atmosphere which can support and nourish a whole community. We do this whenever our thoughts and prayers create forces which we are unable to complete physically so that their activity is predominantly through spiritual realms. When we create forces that we do not complete ourselves, that is repress them, we may have an ever increasing conflict between our desires and feelings to express these forces, and the conditioning and forms needed to contain them. This is explored further in chapter four and five.

As we observe our thoughts and desires we can continually select and empower the best and let go or symbolically or minimally express the negative, cleansing our spiritual being as we do so.

By expressing our unconscious forces in some way whenever we can, we may diminish our personal power to spiritually affect our community or assist or control others. However we will have far greater capacity for acting intuitively in harmony with what our community wants of us or of acting independently of the forces we have created in the past, so that we can be free to be flexible every moment if we wish.

The accumulation of personal power, which we do through all of our conditioning and empowering of our goals or desires, is our way of protecting ourselves from influence and ensuring our effectiveness and success in the future. When we do not identify strongly with a group we trust, we may need to be more powerful to feel that we are secure in the world. As a result, as we collectively diversify and more people attempt to act as individuals, people are becoming more competitive and stressed out. We may need to learn to balance our needs to be individuals with wisdom and compassion for others.

If we have selected for ourselves the unconscious forces we value and if they are organized with only framework parameters and agendas we are free to act in the moment whenever we wish. Our habits, beliefs and routines can be just powerful enough to take care of practicalities while allowing us to change them easily. Our goals and agendas can be confined to what we feel to be of essential importance allowing other aspects of our life to be taken care of by our community, harmoniously. By maintaining this balance in ourselves we enable ourselves to be successful while having enough left to support others as well.

5 Our supraconsciousness.

The essence of all that we experience we make available to our collective, our groupsoul or groupmind. As each of us explores, trains ourselves or imagines possibilities the essences become available to everyone else spiritually. The totality of what is being created or has been created is available to anyone who is resolved to find their way to access it. This totality of possibility can be called our supraconsciousness.

The supraconsciousness is contained in all the beings who are interconnected so that most of what people have access to is contained in the beings of other people. While the contents change each moment it is possible to access both what has been developed in the past and what will be in the future. Some people have a tendency to go to past possibilities while others are always seeking new ones.

What we as individuals contribute to the supra-consciousness depends upon what we involve ourselves in each moment of our lives. What we receive from it is determined by what we are seeking or desiring and have focused our attention on. While we can intuitively receive from the supraconsciousness we may not be able to bring it to consciousness in ourselves, or make use of it, unless we have first prepared foundation skills, knowledge or language in ourselves, for the material to be meaningful to us.

Sometimes what we seek is available but we may intuitively realize that the cost to us of bringing it to consciousness, and reconciling it, may be too great so that it waits in our unconscious until we are ready for it. We may allow it in, in stages or intuitively organize events so that we can experience it in different ways first.

Our imagination, intuition and inspiration are processes of interactions with these spiritual realms. As we develop these we develop our ability to share spiritually.

Most people tap into aspects of our groupmind whenever they explore possibilities without being aware that this is what they are doing. By naturally focusing our attention through thoughts or images, on an area of life and wanting to know or understand more, we may allow new thoughts and possibilities to arise which we can make our own. All that we receive we can flavor and express in a personalized way.

We can experience aspects of our supraconsciousness in different ways according to our own mode of being, the aspect we are acting from, the type of desire that is empowering it, or the nature of the people we are connected to. We can precisely explore ideas, develop skills, create business possibilities or we can imaginatively open up to these realms so that it is as if we fully experience ourselves in them, as in astral travel, being involved in everyday or imaginary activities but in a new way. We can choose where to be participating and to stop being involved there when we wish by moving our attention elsewhere.

6 *Our natural spiritual abilities.*

We all bring our spiritual abilities with us at birth. They are a natural part of being human and through our every experience we develop them further.

In interacting with the physical world and by cooperating in the organization of future events, we intuitively explore and develop our spiritual abilities in a similar way to babies exploring their bodies and muscles. When we want something we will it and then allow our muscles or spiritual abilities to organize themselves to bring it about. Once explored and working well the abilities can continue automatically for years. We can choose to purposefully bring our attention to our spiritual senses as we often do with our tangible senses of movement, smell or touch.

Intuitive performance of skills is less tiring than consciously retraining or learning new ones. If we attempt to consciously control our spiritual abilities excessively, it can also be exhausting and unbalance us.

We may feel our intuition to be a passive ability because in consciousness we may only notice ourselves being still, asking and then feeling out answers to our question. On a spiritual level we may have been extremely active.

With familiarity telepathy and astral travel can be as easy as using our imagination or our memories. It is often the overcoming of the barriers to consciousness which is difficult and exhausting but with practise this gets easier. If we find it exhausting it may be because we have reacted emotionally to what we perceive or because our relationships with the people we shared with, were out of balance.

While we all astral travel intuitively some people are able to consciously direct their attention so that it is as if they are present at the place or with the person they are focusing on. While with them they are able to astrally stand by them and guide them with suggestions or impulses in all they do or assist them in being healed.

It is possible to perceive from a distance everything that another person perceives, creates in their own mind or recalls from the past, or to share anything we have in our own minds. Through the sharing between minds, individuals can influence whole communities, if they are capable enough and creatively assist in the development of their future. Their influence, though, is subject to there already being a need or opening to it. Enabling others to do what they would already like to is easy but to oppose whole communities would exhaust the most powerful individuals.

While it is possible for some people to make instant changes to the world most changes are part of a process that have many steps in it, which all take time. Usually we can only participate and contribute our possibilities rather than create directly, so that the miracle nature of the change may not be seen as such.

If we are considering visiting a friend, an aspect of ourselves may seek her out spiritually, explore her situation and feelings about us, see what she is doing and who is with her. Perhaps we will ask an intuitive aspect of her some questions about what she would like to do and arrange something with her. If she has been open to us and has allowed it to flow through to consciousness she may be able to tell people she is with that we will be coming at a particular time, without knowing how, and if we follow our intuitive agreement we will come at the right moment without knowing ourselves the extent of our involvement.

If we are selling a house we may have many people exploring it astrally and asking intuitive aspects of ourselves questions about it and the price. We might answer everything honestly and voice all of our fears about what could be wrong with the house or we might have prepared in ourselves a very positive view of the house and the price.

Clairvoyantly, we can perceive the spiritual presence of everyone who comes astrally to look at the house, while we are open to it, and we can consciously observe their explorations, some of the decision making process or answer their questions as we choose. Anyone who is blocking the sale for reasons of their own, can be spoken to telepathically and if this fails can be visited physically to clarify their position or to change their involvement. With ethical thoughts and desires harmonious solutions can be found and created to suit everyone.

Many of the premonitions we have are actually spiritual arrangements we have made that naturally come about as agreed. Other premonitions are from the future and usually arrive with a force of their own and are available to people who are open to them without effort or intention.

Premonitions may be a result of our curiosity or concern. If we are seeking particular answers and they are not easily available to us we will naturally seek into the future to gain some insight to prepare us. We may not be conscious of the returning premonition and may need to observe our dreams or allow ourselves to divine the responses so that we might open the right book, turn our radios on or leave home at the right time to hear or find whatever we need to know.

Premonitions can be organized by people at a future moment sending back, wishing to prepare us for an event or be a random resonance with the events themselves.

We are connected to possibilities through time and space and to imaginative or conceptual realms. Just as countries or tourist destinations are always available for us to explore, we can intuitively or consciously direct our attention anywhere or anytime when we choose to, but we may never do so. It may be our vulnerability and fear of being overwhelmed which limits our awareness in spiritual realms.

Intuition, and intuitive astral travel, are active processes that have also been trained by our activities in the physical world. If we are usually focused on physical possessions or places, this is where we will be astrally as well. If we are often exploring goals, concepts and images, then we will astrally share with other like minded people through them. Our spiritual activity is both a cause and a result of where we direct our attention and of the desires and parameters we create.

As we broaden our awareness, gradually become familiar with spiritual possibilities and bring ourselves to balance after each new discovery, we naturally unfold our conscious spiritual perception and creative abilities. Our spiritual development can be a result of our everyday experiences. We are continually preparing ourselves to explore further spiritually whether we bring the process to consciousness or not.

CHAPTER TWO

INTUITIVE LIFE-FORCES

FLOWING THROUGH

A COMMUNITY.

The flow of life as it affects us, intuitively organizes the interactions of the people in a community and arranges events to meet the unfolding of desire forces. It contains forces that set the patterns of change as well as parameters to retain community life in agreed ways, to assist the maintenance of communal harmony.

7 *Life forces flowing through a community.*

On a spiritual level there is a permanent gently nourishing stream of mutual empowerment and influence that flows between us and through our communities. The forces we each assert on the world through our thoughts, desires and intentions, flow out to particular people if directed, and otherwise along habitual pathways. At the same time we are receiving from or through everyone we are connected to, or who focuses on us.

The flow of life force in a community is like the circulation of blood to and through the cells of our bodies. We can take what we need and ignore the rest or we can let it all flow through and transcend the forces as we do so, cleansing the stream. If we are off balance ourselves we can add to the burden that other people receive instead.

With each change in our activities and needs, there is an intuitive movement of our attention through our group-soul by flowing to people, and through our groupmind by flowing through objects of attention that we focus on. As we connect up we draw, give support, seek out or attempt to influence according to our needs, desires or thoughts.

Our attention can be focused and directed to anything we are interested in. We can bring our attention to our physical body and by refining our ability to focus we can come to feel the activity of each cell. Similarly, by refining our attention, it is possible to bring our consciousness into our community and to become spiritually aware of, and interact with, any of the people we focus on.

As the communal stream of life force flows through us we can sample from it. If something meets with a personal imbalance it can cause agitation in us or come to consciousness as something to be dealt with. In meditation we can come to observe or listen to what is causing friction and in the meeting between our own forces and what we receive we can find new insights to assist us to come to harmony in ourselves or with our community.

We may intuitively express the forces at work in us that we have received from others. We can do this directly, as in channeling when we allow forces to flow through us with detachment. However we usually intertwine the forces with our own, through what we are already expressing in our words, thoughts, actions and feelings and in our creative activities.

Some people accept in trust all they receive, expressing both the positive and the negative as it comes to them. They might allow their beliefs, moods, attitudes and goals to be adjusted by what they receive. Other people use discernment to sample from the flow, while assertive people can alter the flow and influence whole communities through their interactions with it.

When we change our roles in our community, or come to be seen differently, the intuitive flow through us also changes as people relate to us differently through their attitudes or the image they hold of us. We can be in the middle of all that happens or be disconnected from the flow. As we change roles we need to adjust our expectations of what we can achieve or influence and be prepared to lose some of the richness of communal life if we give up a role. Many of the activities, relationships or events we participate in, in life, are also about altering the flow of life force to us. Getting "involved" occurs on many levels at once.

If we have many roles, responsibilities or interests, then many of the communities forces may work in us, allowing us to interact or deal with them. If, however, we are focused on our own physical world completely, restricting our interest to it, we may be almost completely detached from what is occurring between people in spiritual realms unless someone focuses directly on us.

Whenever people are complete in an area of life nothing new can come through to influence them. People who are vulnerable, uncertain or trusting can accept or express everything, including illnesses and crimes, on behalf of their group.

Creating new connections with people, or focusing our attention on new areas of life, alters the flow of life force that comes to us to be involved in. We can allow our needs or desires to find new possibilities for us or we can consciously seek them out.

The flow of life as it affects us, intuitively organizes the interactions of the people in a community and arranges events to meet the unfolding of desire forces. It contains forces that set the patterns of change as well as parameters to retain community life in agreed ways to assist the maintenance of communal harmony.

This communal level of the interflow of life-force creates patterns to direct or organize the community just as our personal etheric pattern directs our physical bodies. Just as we can have congestion and depletion in areas of our personal energy body it can occur on a social level as well with some people and groups being well looked after and other individuals or minority groups suffering the imbalances.

Through our groupsoul we are never alone. Twenty four hours a day the people we are connected to may be spiritually available to us, to some extent, and we to them. In times of need we can call, or in times of loneliness know there are others around us or that we can in spirit go to them. If we are closed to consciousness in other realms we may never become aware of this. We may still act and respond according to our needs or the needs of others at times but not be conscious of why.

On going to sleep we can know that those people we have focused on over the last few days, or who have focused on us, may arise. This could occur in clarity or in dream imagery depending on the clarity of our own minds.

By calling people into our dreams and allowing them to participate, our dreams become group creations with many ingredients being shared by everyone, even if the outcomes are perceived in a personal way by each individual. When we become more conscious we can become more aware of the spiritual interactions of other people at anytime and respond to them as we choose.

The spiritual interactions that occur between us are affected by what has previously happened between us physically. The associations these events have created or plans we have for each other will also add to our spiritual involvements with each other. People may see us as a source of assistance or someone they can help, as someone of value or a nuisance. As a result they will attempt to form our spiritual activity and our future behaviour in physical events accordingly.

Imbalanced thoughts, whether of dominance or submissiveness, antipathy or sympathy, authority or deference can lead to complicated astral connections because the individuals are pushed to behave in ways that they feel uncomfortable with.

What we contribute to the flow, affects the response everyone has to us and how happy they will be to participate in what we try to create in our lives. When we wish to improve our relationships with people we can do this through selecting our thoughts and desires that relate to them. Friendly thoughts lead to goodwill and good astral relationships, enabling harmonious groupsouls.

8. *Indications of the flow of spiritual influence.*

We can observe each moment of our lives to see what arises. We can note our own thoughts, feelings and intentions, and the images, suggestions and impulses that come to mind while awake or occurring in our dreams. We can watch all the interplays in our daily physical events. Sometimes we may use divination, telepathy or clairvoyance to observe at a different level and perceive from a distance in space or time.

As we learn to observe we begin to see the interplays between the minds of all the people we are connected to and the collective forces at work flowing through us all.

In our everyday events we can see coincidences, good or ill fortune and patterns or correspondences. Some events enable us to continue in our chosen direction whereas others may block us. Sometimes a series of events leads us to a new group of people or away from an old one unexpectedly. We can observe the changes and if we see the indications early enough we can pause to clarify what our own intentions and parameters are. If necessary we can step in assertively, with our minds and bodies, and contribute in a way that creates events in our life that will suit us better.

The forces of our community flow through everything we are a part of. On a simple level we can have impulses to stay or to go that organize us to be at places at the right time or in the right frame of mind. We can intuitively ask people the right questions that can lead them to share with us unexpectedly enabling something new to arise. At times we will know what they need or what to do for them.

Our intuitive aspects of ourselves, our own knowledge, parameters and goals can interact with the forces of other people and be explored and organized at this level so that when we find a balance, harmony comes intuitively.

As we speak we can observe ourselves choosing one word, idea or an image rather than another or intuitively altering our normal actions and affect our relationship or later events as a result. These may be due to forces from our past, or from our physical needs, stored and expressed unconsciously or triggered by the events around us, as well as from the intuitive flow between us and the other people. These are worth observing as indications of what is occurring within or between us spiritually so that at times we can with wisdom choose anew. This can be for other people's advantage as well as our own.

Everyone intertwines their own chosen words and actions with intuitive ones giving us indications of what else is going on in them or flowing through them. We may have asked ourselves questions which they are answering, perhaps obliquely, for us. At times we may have been thinking about a person lovingly or critically and the next time we see them they begin by intuitively responding to our affection or answering the criticism, about them or someone else.

When we have been observing our thoughts and desires and making a point of noting or remembering them we can find many correlations between what occurs in our minds and what happens around us later, particularly when we are well supported by our community. These events may involve many people who we have never met before.

Telepathically we can have many experiences of the thoughts of other people which are confirmed in what they later do or say. We can astrally perceive people who may be planning to visit or phone us and sometimes we can observe their course long before they arrive. They may have us in mind and be preparing themselves so that in a sense they are already with us. They may be feeling us out, to choose the best time to visit, remembering our mutual past, or wanting to know whether to ask for something they need.

Our dreams can be complete premonitions with details having the clarity of daytime events, or they can be full of the weird and wonderful which we may not see as meaningful as preparations or premonitions, but which we can be reminded of later as events unfold.

Spiritually we can often perceive the forces that are at work but these can be very different from what people finally choose to be a part of. By observing the explorations we can see the options people had and what else was important to them. Everyone changes their minds at times so that their are many possibilities that are shared with our minds that never eventuate.

Often we will participate intuitively when we have agreed to other people's requests, but in addition we can have our own agendas so that everyone can be satisfied. Sometimes, however, the influence on us may be more direct and we may feel pulled along physically as if someone is etherically or astrally present dragging us, and perhaps they are. When we can bring our attention to our energy or etheric level we may feel the touch, push or pull of other people occasionally as they attempt to interact with us. When we can direct our attention spiritually we may be able to perceive who is interacting with us and communicate with them to find out what they think they are doing.

As we become clearer in ourselves it becomes possible to distinguish between what we have created ourselves and express unconsciously, what are random forces that have flowed through our community and what has been created to direct or affect us specifically by another person. We can go with the flow in trust or we can explore what is occurring so that we can discern the intentions of others and choose for ourselves.

Everything that happens on any level comes from someone but much that flows to us from others can be for impersonal reasons. It is not always possible to find the purpose of spiritual interactions but we can come to discern where we are being led at times so that we can choose for ourselves.

9 Different groups and different pathways for the flow.

Each group has a different role in the world just as each member has different roles and needs. This is analogous to the whole of nature or to the cells in our bodies.

Each person's physical body is different with different hormonal balances and different dietary needs. Similarly there are variations between every human group because they focus on different purposes or activities. There are constant but unique expressions into both material and spiritual realms, creating a diversity of possibilities for us to choose from.

Different groups work with different energies and different spiritual forces and orientate themselves to the world in their own way. They have their own balance of chakras and development of spiritual bodies that correspond to their tasks in the world and which enable members to resonate and intuitively co-operate with each other.

All groups have different benefits for humanity and different agendas, inhibitions and needs so that to some extent there is an element of antagonism between any two groups. Without a delineation of membership there could be no opportunity to specialize in a particular area of life or play a particular role.

Some groups are compatible, others actively engage in spiritual warfare with each other, seeing the influence of the other group as our physical body sees an invading organism, something to be conquered or removed.

We usually intuitively find our way to groups that suit us but as we are able to make new choices in all of our encounters, we often connect up to different groupsouls unknowingly. Some new groups will be very supportive while others will create conflicts which can deter us or enable us to address new issues. As a result people are often cautious about joining new groups or becoming intimate with new people, first ensuring that they are from suitable groupsouls or groupminds.

By confining our membership to particular groups we choose the types of intuitive flow of influence or support that we receive. At the same time it is through these people that our forces will flow and if the people are incompatible with us our association may not be fruitful.

People who are able to act from their personal foundations can remain independent from what arrives intuitively. If they wish they are able to temporarily be a part of any group as without an allegiance to a particular group they are not bridges between groups in conflict. By connecting up to different groupsouls or groupminds we are able to participate in different spiritual streams. Every person can lead us to new possibilities which could be challenging but in the process, our life will be enriched.

With self knowledge it becomes possible to be appreciative and tolerant of any person or group, knowing that they have their place in the world and that they too are essential for the unfolding of human destiny.

10 The awakening of independence in changing the flow.

The forces of nature and the cosmos have always flowed through mankind, harmoniously stimulating our development. As mankind began to participate in the creative process, additional spiritual forces came into being.

What a wonderful moment it must have been when the first individuals discovered, as in the Garden of Eden story, that they were able to act in the world independently of what everyone, nature, god, or community, wanted of them, and to cease being intuitively dominated. It became possible to be able to initiate new possibilities and to be creative, acting, thinking and feeling anew each moment rather than always bound by tradition, intuitive expectations, habits or routines.

Human life was able to change, open to new human impulses that could be shared by others or even become universal. Old dangers could be dealt with or prepared for, rather than accepted as inevitable. Mankind was able to begin to explore her potential through exploration of herself in the world.

Coming to personal freedom or individuality would have been gradual with most people still bound by the forces flowing through them with most changes coming from beyond the individual. Gradually more of what an individual did was their own.

Where there may have previously been one person who could initiate change for a whole community, and those changes very few, it became possible for ordinary individuals to have moments of creativity as well.

When individuals began to have their own independent thoughts and actions there came the possibility of conflicts. These could be with other people who disagreed but could also be within the person themselves, as they attempted to make new decisions or cease following old patterns. Being freed from intuitive harmony with nature also created problems, which are forcing us to understand the world in consciousness and to find new solutions with wisdom.

The major forces or influences that direct our lives have been around for a long time and are a part of our inherent nature, common to humanity and a part of the expression of our relationship with the universe. These forces are usually taken for granted and the forces we create are more likely about making minor adjustments in response to what we perceive.

Many people hold an ideal of how humans should behave in every situation. In holding these we empower a form which permanently imposes on people we are connected to, which is effective in forming, shaping or limiting their events.

Every thought and desire we create individually, particularly if a part of a prayer or meditation, affirmation or visualization, is a force acting on other people, with those affected most being those close to us such as friends and family.

Every event that occurs is a result of a range of different forces, from a range of different sources with each person who has an interest in the event or person, asserting their preferences, trying to create the event in their own way.

With greater freedom of thought, and with many individuals asserting themselves and broadcasting a greater number and complexity of possibilities, there came a greater potential for chaos and conflict. It became necessary, in consciousness, to find new methods of creating agreements and harmony.

People have been forced to develop a subtlety in discernment and individual purpose. People could have new impulses, but in consideration of other people, refer them to their community requirements before performing them. Roles were developed giving chosen individuals the rights to make changes in custom or law and other individuals the task of enforcing them.

Laws may be in place now, but the intuitive social organization remains, so that while many people know the consciously imposed laws, they may still live by their intuitively accepted impulses that may have continued for centuries. Tight-knit groupsouls, normal in isolated communities or in family groups, may still operate predominantly through the interflow of intuitive life, despite the conflicts that these unconscious decisions and preferences may cause with the broader community.

All that we have learnt in the past has been added to the collective consciousness or groupmind, whether it is currently of any use or not. There are powerful underground streams intuitively transferred for generations which may not have opportunities for fruitful expressions or adjustments. These streams of patterning can wait to be expressed for centuries until a possibility of a cultural renaissance arises. They can remain for centuries after their usefulness is over, and be behind the activities of mafia style groups or some religious cults.

Many of the organized migrations of people of modern times, has been a part of a political agenda of a breakdown of the power of intuitive groupsoul forces, on people. Everyone is being forced to refer their behaviour and thoughts to what they are taught, know or perceive physically or consciously, rather than from what they intuitively know or receive. This enhances the possibilities of social conformity or rapid change being organized through physical events or training and removes some of the spiritual barriers to change.

While our choices may come to be dominated by physical considerations the intuitive forces are much a part of what humanity is as a collective. In times of doubt, on an individual or collective level, it is always these intuitive forces and mechanisms that provide the new alternative or organize our behaviour.

In times of clarity we can adjust these collective forces to ensure that they remain relevant to our changing world. The explorations and strivings of every individual can contribute to this development.

11 Indirect and random flows in a community.

While astral contacts may be direct with a particular person focused on, or astrally visited, etheric contacts and flows can be quite different. These appear to operate at a deeper level organizing our physical behaviour and actions without our consciousness.

Many people who have an idea, desire or suggestions for change, may not associate it with particular people so that there can be a random flow, like an electrical flash finding its way to its destination, along any means available. Entering the collective can be like entering a maze as our attention and forces may not flow directly and it may not be possible to identify who is responding.

Each person we focus on can be a channel for others. Sometimes people focus on other people without a direct connection, praying for someone's mother or sending disapproval to a friend's spouse or boss so that the effect has to flow through the person they do know and it could be spiritually perceived as coming from them instead. People may in support be sending impulses, prayers or images to their friends and family but the ones who they are meant for may be unaffected by them, letting them flow past to other people who can use them.

When people wish to change the world or some of the people in it, their created and empowered forces may radiate through everyone they know, or who focuses on them, flowing through people who find the suggestions meaningless to people who can express them or who will resist or transform them.

A request for a job could flow through many people before one is found and then it needs to be relayed back.

When a person is clearly focused about who they are and what they want they will have more success as it can be more direct and avoid confusion.

All people create spiritual forces to some extent, for a range of purposes, and these forces are continually flowing through everyone's beings, usually unconsciously, until they can be completed. The process may be similar to the personal one of searching for an answer or worrying where the thoughts go backwards and forwards until a solution arises. The difference is only one of scale.

When a community has particular needs, these can become focused in particular individuals who can unexpectedly arise to meet the communities challenges, whether great or small.

Many of the forces that are transferred between people are done so symbolically or analogically. The essence of many desires, concepts, feelings can be quickened to the same image or symbol which can be transferred between people far more easily than the whole story. Our minds often do this automatically as a means of organizing material.

In traditional homogeneous communities, symbols may have had the same meaning for everyone so that intuitive guidance was uncomplicated. The impulse created by one person would usually have been expressed by someone else in the expected way. These days with the diversity of possible meanings as well as of personal preferences, forces which we create for others, if expressed at all will be in a personalized way.

The longevity of the forces means that many of the forces we encounter in life may have flowed through hundreds of people before we feel the impulse at the moment of possibility of being completed. When we consider all the options that are available we can imagine or feel a complicated ebbing and flowing of life forces through us.

12 Interacting with the flow of life forces through us.

When we allow everything to flow through or be expressed through us we are participating in the communities unfolding without altering it. When the community is healthy this can be a harmonious way to live. However the flow of influence or support through us can be used both to be nourished or inspired ourselves or to inspire others through our personal involvement in all we do.

When we refine ourselves and our understanding in any area of life we can become confident about it. If an attitude, area of knowledge or skill is often in our mind with confidence or certainty, then this is what we broadcast to the world, and this is how we will be flavoring all that flows through us.

Whether the creation is in art, science, invention or ideas a creator directs themselves to be able to receive from an aspect of their collective mind, to select from it and to combine what they receive, with their own forces, in a creative way. Good art flows from the people to the creative person who can express it, spiritually, and then, through their activities, returns to the physical realm for others to experience it there, bringing something to consciousness in each of the participants.

Each creator can reflect the community mind that they are a part of. Much of what they create will have a meaning to their personal group and its value depends on both the spiritual influence they are a part of, as well as their own discernment and ability.

Some creative people work almost completely from their trained personal foundations and allow very little that is new through. Others are so open to collective forces that what they create may be completely unpredictable and in extreme cases they can be the hands for other people to spiritually work or be channeled through. In creative activities we can allow ourselves to be open, even gullible, at first, so that new forces and possibilities can arise and be expressed through us, and then we can use discernment to select what is of value and to contribute our own forces at the same time.

An artist can lift art in their community by being dedicated to their art, even if their work is little seen by their local community. Everyone that focuses on them in any way can be influenced or inspired. The artists mind may be permanently filled with particular soul qualities that can enable other people to appreciate life in a new way.

If we create for a particular purpose, writing a healing story for a person, creating a statue for a church or memorial, or writing a book for a new age, we can focus ourselves on the interested individual or community to allow their forces to participate in our creative process.

Anyone who comes to a fuller understanding of a field of life, whether physical or spiritual, can create an impulse that will spread through humanity. If it is of value, it can be amplified in acceptance by people rather than be transformed, and a new social movement can come into being through an underground stream.

13 Bringing the flow to consciousness.

To distinguish personal intuition from the flow requires self knowledge, and an awareness of what our mind has been doing. Often at the moment of expression we are not concerned about where the possibilities come from but whether they are of any value. With clarity, consciousness of transpersonal flows can come directly. We can experience aspects of them with our minds as we would physical experiences, knowing their source as separate to us. Transpersonal forces can also be experienced in dreams, received visualizations, externally projected as with visions and hallucinations, or they can be observed as we or others express the forces at work into the physical world.

The forces that flow through us can be actively created in the mind of someone as we receive it but often they are created at random without any consciousness of us and they await a moment of possibility. What occurs on the spiritual level plants the seeds of possibility within us so that a simple word, image, action or gesture can bring it through into consciousness.

The spiritual preparations can be trivial or organize major life changes for us or our community. The forces can be at work for months or years while we unconsciously participate with them until the moment of action comes when we may suddenly realize what it is we have been involved in. We may choose a moment that ensures success and have an easy transition between partners, jobs or towns, or a moment that is inappropriate and spares us the change or aborts it. Other people will often attempt to induce the moment of change for us so that the timing is to their benefit.

To come to understand spiritual realms we can first develop an awareness of the many different patterns occurring in every day life and of the effects of all of our thoughts and desires on events. A person who understands the unconscious forces at work in their community can with a minimum of effort or display, bring about major changes.

When the forces waiting to be expressed find people who have no resistance to them, they will flow through freely. If one person resists them, it often happens that the material finds someone else to express it.

The material world is the expression of what has previously been explored, decided and empowered in other realms by the collective. Changes in material realms require preceding changes in spiritual realms and once a situation or aspect of reality has been fully accepted and found its own harmony, the impulses to change may cease. As a result any forces for change are most effective during times of uncertainty in the individual or community.

Each person takes the new positions and patterns deeply into their conditioned body, where they can impose them automatically and resist or ignore any new forces. In consciousness we can set aside our conditioning, reject new forces working on us and choose anew.

CHAPTER THREE

CONNECTIONS AS

PATHWAYS FOR

THE FLOW.

Imbuing all of life, all people, animals, plants and rocks, is an etheric energy patterning which empowers and assists in the organization of the physical components of life. Our spirits can connect up and interact with any part of this patterning and our forces can contribute to the creation of possibilities for future changes or events that the person or object we are focused on is involved in.

14 What are spiritual connections

A spiritual connection is a possibility we create for a flow of life-energy or influence between us and another person or object of attention.

Imbuing all of life, all people, animals, plants and rocks, is an etheric energy patterning which empowers and assists in the organization of the physical components of life. Our spirits can connect up and interact with any part of this patterning and our forces can contribute to the creation of possibilities for future changes or events that the person or object we are focused on is involved in.

When we focus our intention, or our intuitive forces flow through naturally, we contribute to the enablement of a change. Ours are only some of the forces at work, even if the final ones. If our spiritual activity is at the right time, and supported by other active spiritual forces, it can enable a change to occur at the etheric level immediately which can flow through to an instant physical change.

The changes we can influence or support through our connections, can include any of life's changes at any level, anywhere. How effective we are in influencing changes is dependent on our own purpose, clarity, power or community support. We can enable changes in ourselves, other people, our community or the world around us.

Through our connections we can influence changes in anyone's health, relationships and jobs, or changes in people's beliefs and goals. We can also suggest changes in the weather or create patterns for new community projects.

Connections can be momentary or we can reinforce them until they become habitual so that flows of power and influence can continue intuitively through them at any moment of our life.

We might focus most of our attention on people, on nature, our physical possessions, or on our work tasks. It is through whatever we focus our attention on that we relate to the world. To remove or alter the area of our lives that we habitually focus on alters the flow of life that we can be a part of, interact with or be nurtured by.

By focusing our attention we interact spiritually with everything we perceive. If we do this with any interest, desire or aversion, we are creating connections to whatever we are focused on. The connections may be temporary or permanent, weak or strong, sources of joy or of conflict.

We can love or support people in compassion, or accept from them gratefully, without making a habitual connection. Connections require a level of continuing interest before they will be maintained intuitively, after we move our conscious attention away.

As we become more familiar with someone or something we also create a permanent intuitive link to everything under their scope. While it may not come to consciousness we may often know much that is occurring in our community and intuitively fit in with it or make use of what we have learned.

Once we have connected to someone or something we can spread our attention, open up and become aware of and accept or deal with whatever we find there. We all can come to live with the support and assistance of our groupsoul or groupmind and can use our intuition or consciously act in the world with the resources of a group whenever necessary. In turn we are all a part of a group supporting others spiritually.

When we move our attention we alter the flow between ourselves and the world. As we alter our attitude we alter our relationship to who or what we focus on. We can exhaust ourselves on trying to change people through criticism or antagonism or support them with goodwill. We can open up to people and be nurtured and brought into alignment with the forces at work, or we can be detached about what we receive.

As long as we have thoughts and desires in our minds we are consciously flowing to whatever we are focused on as well as taking new forces into ourselves. When we provide the energy our intuitive personal forces that we had begun in the past, can be at work in an attempt to come to completion.

While some forces flow through us at all times, in stillness, with our will disengaged, it becomes possible for forces of people we are connected to, to flow through us, to others, without our involvement or interference.

While people may be the main source and destination of our spiritual flows, it is also possible to connect our minds indirectly to them, whether we know them or not, through people, leaders, objects, places, symbols, images, ideas, beliefs, memories, goals or any shared interest or temporarily through anything we both focus our attention on.

We can connect to many people through resonances between intuitive aspects of each of us. How broad-ranging our connections can be in life depends on how broad our interests, foundations and unconscious forces are.

Our spiritual activity or exploration is only limited by what we are able to connect up to. As our familiarity or awareness of the world increases we become able to connect up or interact with it more fluidly. As we become more aware in spiritual realms we are able to become more subtle or effective in what we perceive or create there.

How we connect up to different parts of the world and the aspect of ourselves we do it with determines how we experience it. We can perceive physically, etherically, astrally or clairvoyantly according to how we are focusing our attention. Just as we can activate our sense of smell, we can also bring our spiritual perceptions to consciousness at will when we have learnt to.

We can open up, explore and be conscious of who there is currently interacting spiritually with us. This observation can be as the events are being created in their minds, as we intuitively interact with them in their attempts to include us in their agendas or as the influences are expressed in physical events.

It is not possible to focus on someone or something without spiritually interacting with them and to a lesser extent, everyone else they are connected to. Due to the inter-connections, and the flow between everyone, what we receive needn't come from the person we are focused on but can be from beyond them.

We can empower or draw power or influence from anything we are focused on, each time we focus on them. In times of need we can give intuitive support or draw from everything and everyone we are habitually connected to. In doing so we affect to some extent the unconscious aspects of all those people who flow with us.

Usually we will receive from the surplus that is available but in times of need we may drain people, who are supportive of us, to their detriment. When we create a surplus in ourselves we can give the surplus to anyone who needs to draw in, enabling them to come to balance or completion in some area or to pass the life energy on.

Just as we can connect up to particular types of people through our interest in nature, our profession or types of ideas, we can also tune into new possibilities or areas of interest through a powerful connection to a person. To marry into a family of artists will usually mean that we will have access to impulses and suggestions about art. Obviously we would need to have the personal foundations in place that could meet the suggestions, to make use of them.

Our spiritual connections to people can be created through objects of attention or other people long before meeting them. On a groupsoul level we may come to know each other well before being conscious of each others existence, so that as soon as we meet we may be comfortable with each other and have intuitively organized our relationships.

By focusing on parts of our body we can feel or create changes there in our life-energy or muscles and organs. Once we have learnt to focus on people or objects we can consciously become aware of the changes there too.

Whether we are aware of it or not we create a possibility for people to change each time we focus on them as our own forces can intuitively flow through. We could also receive from them or share with them and feel their joys, desires, inhibitions or imbalances, in sympathy.

If we are consciously receptive we can feel or sense people each time they are focused on us and be aware of their thoughts or any images or suggestions they were sending. We could in reply communicate with them according to our style, verbally or through images or impressions or we could feel their impulses through our bodies. When we are aware of people we needn't respond to what they may be projecting, we can choose our own response or create an image of ourselves waving in friendship to them.

With spiritual perception our awareness and participation in life can go to new levels. This is a natural part of our human potential that we can all awaken to if we organize our lives and prepare ourselves for it.

15 *Our intuitive selection of spiritual influences.*

Through our connections we can give or receive a diversity of influences or possibilities. We can be empowered directly by a gift of life-energy from someone sharing with us or have evoked in us a state of mind through which we empower ourselves or let go of the fears and blockages to the natural flow of life-energy.

Sometimes the influence we receive can create conflict and fear in us so that we feel a loss of energy as a result. If we are too open to someone, we can have our surplus life-energy removed to them and in some cases we can be drained to the point of ineffectiveness.

We all have trained ourselves to have a natural selection process which protects from unwanted influences, while allowing the natural beneficial flow to continue. We learn to choose who to be open to, how far to be open to them and what type of influence to accept. This selection process continues intuitively all the time and is organized by our etheric body. We can adjust our connections in consciousness as we review relationships or intuitively as we have new experiences.

Our selection process can be a result of our choice of friends or associates or through the creation of our personal foundations and areas of interest. It can also be through our membership of a group that intuitively protects us and selects and filters what can become available to us.

Spiritual influence can come through this natural armouring according to our chosen paths of support and influence, so that our patterns and thoughts are still unexpectedly changed. Where the influence comes through our connections to our groupsoul it is a means of keeping us in alignment with our group. Someone else may have created or allowed in a new spiritual influence as a result of their physical or spiritual experiences and it is being shared around intuitively.

When we are part of a group we will be protected by the group or leader who can intuitively transform or transcend everything that comes to the group which is inappropriate. In turn the group's forces, goals and parameters, will be imposed on us to keep us in alignment and prevent us from creating adverse influences for others.

If we have an attitude of acceptance or surrender to life we may always be protected by our group and not need to deal with many conflicts ourselves. Where people belong to a homogeneous community they can have faith in their future unfolding naturally. They can accept all that they are a part of knowing that the dynamics of the group, its leader and its relationship to the world, will ensure that everything will be beneficial to them.

If we wish to be free from the constant intuitive realignment by our group, we need to create our own personal armouring. We can do this by establishing personal foundations that everything can be checked against.

When we are clear in who we are and what we are about, we will intuitively deal with anything that we receive and only the material that creates conflict, or is in doubt, will need to arise to consciousness, to be addressed.

When we are part of a homogeneous group it is as if everything has been addressed by others already and there is little need for further personal assessment.

If we spend time with people who belong to a different groupsoul and open up to them we can be easily influenced but we can be brought back into alignment by spending time with some of our own groups anchormen who have strong personal foundations. In many communities this was one of the roles of the religious services, or rituals, so that people who had been caught up in range of new possibilities during the week could intuitively realign with their group again.

If we have yet to establish personal foundations of habitual responses, beliefs, attitudes, goals and allegiances, we may wish to avoid unsuitable influences. We may attempt to cut off from many people but this approach also cuts us off from much of the natural inter-flow of life as well as the natural protection through being part of a group. We would need to make all choices in consciousness until our personal armouring was complete and operated intuitively once more. The burden of living at this level of awareness is too exhausting for most people.

By focusing our attention, even if against the will of our groupsoul, on new areas and interests, new spiritual influences or groups, (including football teams if that is our desire) we create a new set of spiritual influences to be involved in and from which we can come to choose anew each moment. Our selection mechanism would have opened up to allow in a lot of new material and possibilities and can free us from the exclusive direction of old groupsouls. This new field of possibilities can be daunting at first until we become used to the process of conscious discernment and selection and begin to know ourselves as separate from our families, employer, role or old groups.

This selection mechanism or armouring has a spiritual reality in the form of an etheric sheath or veil which participates in the organizing of every activity we engage in. All of our habitual responses and rhythmical activities are alive at this level.

In times of uncertainty, illness or trauma we weaken this armouring so that we are more vulnerable to what flows through. Our habitual responses, and even skills, or memories, can all be lost through a disturbance to our etheric sheath and as a result we are inclined to accept any suggestion which reaches us. In times of confidence, strength or single-mindedness we transform much that we receive or interact with into our own patterning so that we affect everyone we are connected to, who is open, instead.

Our personal foundations interact with all that we perceive physically and determine how we allow ourselves to be affected. The process of assimilating what we experience can be carried out for years as we come to terms with it or open up to its influence. What we accept intuitively however, will alter our patterns immediately or create conflict.

When we express the change in our patterns we can observe our new behaviour or thought and make a conscious decision and choose whether to keep it or not. These changes are often of value with us intuitively developing new knowledge or skills as well as new beliefs and goals.

All of our interactions through our connections are opportunities for us to bring our personal forces from our conditioned or desire bodies, to balance or completion. We may experience it as a conflict but by dealing with it we come to choose and know who we are. In confidence we can open up broadly to life knowing that we are able to discern and choose again if necessary.

16 Our historical connections with our families.

The strongest personal connections are usually the habitual ones we have from birth or with or own children. Not only are these powerful due to the amount of shared experiences, genetic similarities and natural resonances, but also because the relationships are usually so enmeshed that it is often difficult to know for certain which thoughts, beliefs, feelings, goals or inhibitions are truly ours and which we have taken on and not explored yet.

The spiritual connections between family members are usually solid and powerful. Many of our memories, particularly the unconscious ones of early childhood, were created with these people. Consciously or otherwise we are reminded of them constantly, creating a flow between us each time and strengthening our connections with them in the process.

Our involvement with our family and people we grew up with, can be a source of support and reassurance. All the similarities in beliefs, goals and values, can enable us to relate with these people with intuitive harmony. In times of vulnerability or need we can be nurtured by these people without having to deal with a lot of unwanted influences.

There are, however, challenges that arise through our historical connections for individuals who are attempting to create their own, personal foundations. There is always an attempt at creating intuitive realignments through these connections to maintain harmony in the groupsoul, and these are at a level that it is difficult to become conscious of.

While our family connections are powerful, they are almost always out of balance with many parent/child, helper/victim, leader/follower type relationships persisting throughout life and long after death. As a result there can be unnecessary subservience to people who's influence we have no need of, or desire for.

With many modern family members living at a distance to each other, family relationships rarely keep up with all of our personal life changes. The images our families have of us are often of how we were long ago or of how they expected us to turn out. Primitive tribes with their rites of passage avoided this problem as each change was simple, precise and acknowledged by everyone. An individual could redefine themselves with each change, and the rites allowed all the connections an individual had with their community to be altered in a harmonious way, at the one time.

As a result of the modern absence of rites of passage

the old psychic forces imposed on us by our families can continue and through these our families attempt to direct or hold us in an inappropriate way. To overcome these influences far more effort may need to be made to impress on people that a change has been completed. The lack of easy agreement about our changes can lead to power battles, emotional scenes or even separations, as a way of forcing an acknowledgment of the change, and a removal of the pressure to return to a past arrangement. As we are more open to our families we are also more easily intuitively influenced by them and have greater difficulty in altering our relationships with them.

By making preparations for alterations in how we relate in our own mind first we will be clearer in demonstrating our new image and our determination in it. We can then allow others to replace the old image of us or let go of the relationship. Being secure in our new foundations can make us less vulnerable to pressure to change again.

Understanding the processes of change in our children and periodically choosing to let go, parents can alter their relationships and expectations to more suitable ones. By expanding our images of our children as they grow older, to encompass anything they may wish to do and be, we can still empower them personally without setting their agendas. We can change our role to that of a friend or resource person rather than the teacher, dictator or helper we were.

Powerful parents who do not detach from their children and continue to pray for or want particular outcomes can continue to psychically organize their children for the rest of their life, without being consciously aware of it. These people can be the permanent guides of their children and can be spiritually perceived as standing behind them at any moment of change or uncertainty.

17 Connections through resonance with our soul qualities.

Our natural connections can be based on the whole of our beings or on any part of it. The soul qualities we brought with us at birth, or have developed at any time since if they are still alive in us, or that we will unfold in the future, can be distilled or quickened to an essence on a spiritual level. We are able to intuitively connect up with or respond to people who have an attraction to us through a natural resonance with these essential qualities and aspects.

We can be attracted to these people through who or what they are. We can find people we resonate with us anywhere in the world independently of having to experience anything with them and we may feel an intuitive kinship with them. The resonance may be a result of a common source or spiritual stream, qualities and values, through shared conditioning, interest, family, language, fear, aversion, beliefs, goals, religion or culture. In a sense all of these are expressions of an essential mood or quality that has unfolded further through our experiences.

It may have been our destiny, through our essential nature, to be attracted to a community of people with particular qualities, so that ours could be completed or developed further. Our essential nature will automatically and unconsciously arrange our life so that we can meet the people with whom we can create the events and experiences we need to fulfil ourselves.

There may be an automatic meeting of minds with people through being on the same wavelength. Some people call people with whom they relate to in this way their soul mates. When we resonate with a person it is quite different to a common connection through an object or third person. We can feel it with every part of our being.

We have a whole range of interests, desires and needs that we interact with the community through. We can also choose, in consciousness, to operate from any of our aspects and can evoke in people responses from different aspects of them. If we meet people while in an aspect of ourselves that we can share together then our relationship can flow easily.

An ex-roman catholic may have a resonance with roman Catholics for years after he has left the religion. Aspects of his being were empowered by his involvement in the religion and these aspects remain available for resonance until they are changed or removed. Catholics may intuitively attempt to evoke these aspects in relating to him.

In resonating with some aspect of a person it is as if we are already together and our forces can cooperate and flow easily. Whether we meet them physically or not there can be a flow between us on spiritual levels.

We make many of our connections with people long before we meet so that the meeting is only the beginning of conscious involvement. Having a natural attraction to someone which enabled our meeting, doesn't mean that our relationship in the physical world will be meaningful. What we need to do together may be completed in minutes or years, with or without intimacy or obligations being involved. We can choose our level of involvement or what to do with any influence we receive.

When an individual is involved in an area of life, what they perceive or discover is shared through their groupmind with anyone who resonates with it naturally, or is focused on it through their interests. Through the groupmind people can develop a field of knowledge, artistic endeavor or invention and participate in a project together even if only one of them is consciously expressing it into the physical world.

Those people who can fit into our agendas or destiny, will be attracted or pulled into our lives without us needing to be concerned how, although we can come to consciousness in transpersonal realms if we wish. Any perception, desire, criticism or possibility can flow through a community of people through a common resonance.

In a sense all of our connections to people are a result of a need for completion so that once our imbalances are dealt with we may have no need for new connections or even to hang on to the old ones. As we live we gradually alter what we resonate with and the people and experiences we will attract to ourselves in this way.

18 Connections through a common focus of attention.

When we focus on something, whether we are conscious of it or not, it is as if a part of us goes out to it and is there with it. This happens whether we see it with our physical eyes or our spiritual senses. If we have become familiar with something it is as if a part of us remains with it. As other people connect to the common object of attention, whether physical, emotional or mental, it is as if we are there together. We spiritually have it in common.

Any person, object, place, symbol, idea, image, memory, ritual, future event, sensation, emotion, or shared goal that we are attached to or focused on, enables us to be connected to others who are connected to it as well. The common focus enables many people, who may otherwise have no relationship, to be connected temporarily.

In some cases where people have shared powerful experiences, such as wars or other disasters, or have been part of an exciting course of personal development or training, there can be a permanent connection without the people having met. They could become kindred spirits through their common experience, and know it intuitively on meeting.

Connections through a common object of attention can be used in many areas of life where people requiring assistance to invent, to know, to learn and even to heal, can focus on what they need and receive assistance from people who have already travelled the same road. Many new discoveries are a collective affair on a spiritual level, gaining contributions from many people until it is completed in the minds of them all, even if only expressed completely by one of them.

If a person has the foundation skills or understanding they can be assisted to perform far beyond their previous personal best, intuitively finding creative solutions to any problem that may arise, or intuitively finding their way to appropriate books, courses or people when they need to bring something to consciousness.

To develop a new ability in any area of life we need to stay with it to gradually expand our foundations while creating new intuitive connections to people who are also involved in it and are pulled in through our interest. We may connect to the right people before having prepared ourselves to be able to make use of what they have available so that our intuitive training can be in advance of our conscious ability to express it.

Our groupmind is contained in the minds of all the people who share our interest. As we focus on an idea, image or symbol it is as if our minds are intuitively flickering through the minds of others seeking material dealing with areas we are focusing our attention on. If we stay with the object of attention then we may spiritually interact with the people sharing it so that we overlap into other areas of their life as well and may attract them into the physical events of our life. Through shared interests or agendas we pull new people into our lives.

The names we are called can tune us in to people accidentally who are seeking people with the same name as ours. We can also receive the good will or suggestions meant for a person of the same name. When we focus on a person with a particular name it helps avoid confusion if our focus is precise and in our thoughts we have a clear image as well as a full name. If we have a precise memory of a person we can have a telepathic link with them anywhere in the world.

Sometimes our broadcasts can be to everyone who is open to us so that people who have focused on us or are astrally present or open to us habitually, may organize people with the same name accidentally instead. These people can come to be involved, express the influence, or act out the impulse.

Memories shared by people who participated in positive events, can evoke a commonalty or safety area for them all, so that harmony is more easily possible. When a person remembers, he creates associations with the people and events or places in the memory, so that a flow occurs easily. The people in the memory may have an image of the rememberer or the event at the same time.

When the object of attention is a leader, dead, alive or imaginary, a person can connect himself to people who are focusing on the same leader and be in communion with them.

It is as if a spiritual being is being created by the leader and followers that can come to have a degree of independence from all of them, and which can continue after the death of the leader. This is part of the power of a spiritual leader. He is able to create a new groupmind and groupsoul which any member of the group can relate to and assist or be nourished from. The being of the leader comes to embody a particular set of qualities that can be evoked in the individuals by connecting up to the image of him.

The leader, or what his followers create of him after death, becomes the focus point through which cooperation and support can flow. The patterns, moods or qualities that are created, guide the nature of the influence that flows when people focus on his image or do a visualization of him.

Jesus Christ is a creation of the collective mind now quite independent from the person who once lived. The interpretation of who Christ is changes with each century and varies between each group that focuses on him despite efforts of new leaders to codify his qualities.

If the leaders are appropriate for their time, their influence will grow and enable their community to benefit the world but if their spiritual influence is of the past they will hold their community back. As there is a diversity of people in the world there is also a need for a diversity of spiritual influences so that what may be outmoded for one individual may still be relevant to others.

When a leader's spiritual influence continues to grow after their death, and comes to be available to the whole world, such as with a Christ or a Buddha, an uplifting universal consciousness becomes available, through which people are able to find spiritual guidance and harmony.

19 Connections to physical objects.

When we focus our minds on obtaining, or disposing of a material object, people connected to the object, or seeking it out, will be temporarily connected to us enabling our lives to be organized so that an exchange of the object can take place.

Some people follow all the logical routes to meet their desires, whereas others empower their desires, pray and believe god will provide or surrender to the cosmos, and then wait for it to arrive. Understanding the processes that follow the creation of our thoughts and desires, people can intuitively cooperate with their community in their physical activities. A response will come if there is a possibility that also suits other people.

If an object has been lost, unavailable or in an irretrievable position the owner in yearning for it may continue their connection with it and find a way back to the object once it becomes available again. Empowered events and objects are like repressed thoughts or forgotten dreams, waiting on the edge of consciousness for their chance to be acknowledged again, our connections to them may be always working to bring them back.

If we have made a connection to a place or object it is possible for any association with it to take us there in memory but we can also bring our attention there astrally so that our consciousness can be there at the moment of the association. Our memories are fixed to the time of day we were there but when we return astrally we may notice the time, the weather or surroundings changed.

We may become very attached to our bed. On one level whenever we relax anywhere in the world we may feel ourselves back in it. When someone else focuses on the bed they can find aspects of us there as we are habitually connected to it with part of our intuitive attention. If they wish they can communicate with us through our connections to our bed or our house.

Through our connections to animals it is possible to sense through the animal, to direct it and to observe what is occurring elsewhere, as witches were reputed to do but which any person with a pet could do accidentally. Animals do not have the ego strength that people have and are accepting of human involvement in their lives. They will attempt to obey or cooperate with us whether the instructions are verbal or from our desires through images.

It is also possible to connect up to a letter to perceive in places, even overseas, where one has never been before. Through someone else's letter or possessions we can intuitively know much about their lives as it is a direct link to them.

20 Flows through our connections to physical objects.

When we reach out to find anything intuitively it is as though we do it through everyone and everything we are connected to until we find what we are looking for, in a similar way to scanning through our memory. How successful we are in locating things or ideas depends on what we are initially focused on or where our attention would naturally flow through associations with our objective.

The flow continues at all times whether we are conscious of it or not so that anything we are focused on, with our physical senses, our thoughts, imagination or memory, will be a bridge for a flow.

If we constantly look at a neighbors house or car because it is in front of our window, we may also be interacting with the neighbor even if we haven't met. Some people maintain a continuing attachment to their house or car. Through this connection we can come to have a feeling about the kind of life that goes on it or share their joys, fears and interests.

Any thief focused on our house with an intention to rob us focuses on us as well if we are attached to it, so that we can intuitively know to go home and get there before the thief breaks in. We are able to feel out possibilities through time as well so that we can organize the timing of our arrival.

Anyone can visit us astrally through their natural curiosity. Just because we have astral visits from people it does not mean we need to be connected. We may live in a house that many people are curious about so that many strangers explore the house, and us in the process, and we can acknowledge them without needing to have anything further to do with them.

If we see an advertisement for a room to rent we can allow ourselves to feel it out intuitively to see if it feels right or not. The conscious result can be very simple with us either feeling good about it or not. The actual process, however, is far more complicated as we astrally find our way to the room, explore it, the house and the people in it and our possible future there and make up our mind from the impressions we receive. A clairvoyant living in the house could observe our astral presence and communicate with us encouraging us to come or to stay away.

It is common to astrally meet up with people through places we have lived in and that they remember us in. New people living there can become aware of us whenever we are remembering it. We can also meet up with people through places we would like to live in as we go there astrally.

The familiarity we have with our roots enables us to resonate with them and the people there easily. We can be nurtured through connections with our hometowns so that in times of difficulty we may wish to go home, for the people but also for the nurturing effect the place can have on us.

We can be connected to people through any physical object we share. Lovers often intuitively wear each other's clothes and at times can feel as if they are both wearing them at once. They may also leave some clothes at each other's houses to have another avenue for a connection.

Gifts that people give or experiences they share can connect people for life even if they have little natural affinity for each other. In order to establish relationships giving gifts and having special times together are very powerful means. Each time we see the present we can be opening ourselves up to the giver through the associations the gift evokes. By often thinking of our friends in a positive way we are strengthening our links with them.

Well selected photos can assist us in focusing on members of our groupsoul in a positive way. In remembering we are also creating as we can empower whatever we have in mind. By remembering the positive aspects or qualities of a person we are empowering the image we impose on them in a positive way. We can all contribute to creating a positive spiritual environment that we can all live in.

In this chapter, I have described different kinds of connections; unilateral ones, where one person focuses on a person or object, bilateral ones where two people are connected directly and collective connections where many people share together through a common focus or ritual. These can all occur intuitively although consciousness for everyone is possible.

Most spiritual connections are mutually beneficial as they expand our possibilities in life. If the conflict between the essences of the people is too great they can be exhausting due to the struggle to reconcile the differences.

Eventually all people, all beings and even all things are connected but effectively we are only powerfully connected to people we are related to, share something with or have something we commonly resonate with.

In any city we can find people who have something in common with us but not with the other million people. The groups are like threads in a tapestry with only occasional contacts between them.

As we change our goals, beliefs, parameters or interests we will automatically begin to connect up with new people and let go of some old ones. Each change we are a part of leads us to new possibilities of exploring and unfolding new aspects of ourselves.

CHAPTER FOUR

EXPLORING THE FLOW

WITHIN AND BETWEEN

INDIVIDUALS.

The dynamic of individual health and even morality, is a group one, so that our well-being, states of mind, self image, as well as our life and financial successes, are created through the dynamic spiritual interactions between ourselves and other people.

As our consciousness grows it becomes possible to interact with people completely through spiritual realms. We can respond to what they communicate to us spiritually or from what we observe of them spiritually.

21 Our spiritual bodies

Imbuing our physical body we have spiritual bodies which we can feel within ourselves or experience in activity in spiritual realms. We can feel the flow of our etheric body through our physical body and in relaxing or meditating we can enable it to bring our physical body into alignment with its patterning.

We may discover the activities of our astral body by observing the impressions we retain after feeling people or situations out. We could consciously find our attention at a distance or we can learn to purposefully astral travel. If we create desires and parameters we can also observe how our astral and etheric bodies organize events. At times we will perceive the spiritual activities of other people.

Our etheric body intuitively forms or directs our activities and can be trained or conditioned. Our astral body wants to lead us out into the world to fulfill our destinies, our egos, or "I"s, empower and direct our spiritual bodies and their coordination of our physical body. Our H.selves can come to mediate in consciousness between our own spirit's needs and those of our community.

As we become familiar with an area of life we take the essence of what we learn, accept or choose, into our etheric or conditioned body, and create patterns with which we will organize our future activities and relationships with the world.

Once trained we can act intuitively so that most of what we are involved in can continue without our conscious attention. Our etheric body will look after the health of our physical body, coordinate our activities with habits and routines, hold our beliefs, attitudes, skills and abilities and be our automatic pilot in any familiar situation.

Through our habitual relationships, our etheric body is intimately connected to our groupsoul so that intuitively it is being constantly adjusted or protected from change. While we have the main role and responsibility, our health and well-being is a co-operative affair with our groupsoul looking after us at all times if necessary.

Our astral body has many qualities. It is the yang or assertive aspect of our spiritual forces. It is also the name for our collection of desires that organize our futures through which we attempt to make the world in our own image.

We can consciously choose whether to empower forces, from other people, acting on our astral or etheric bodies or choose to redirect them or to let them go. By choosing in consciousness with discernment, we enable our " I " to be involved in organizing and stimulating our etheric and astral bodies and through them to create our own lives and the effect we have on the world.

Our " I " is our Ego or Spirit. Our physical, etheric and astral bodies are the vehicles through which our spirits can fulfill themselves or complete their destinies. Our egos work through our desire and conditioned bodies to assert our forces on the world or interact with the forces of other people. These forces can be co-operated with and empowered by other people, or redirected or blocked in their interactions with us, making our spiritual activities less effective.

Egotism is usually a consequence of an imbalanced desire body, dominating our ego. Strong balanced Egos enable us to have what we need in life while cooperating with other people to everyone's benefit.

With each experience we have we can evoke in ourselves an interest for greater involvement now or in the future. We can empower our astral body by actively dwelling in it and enable it to explore and co-ordinate future events through which our desires can be satisfied or completed.

When we direct our attention elsewhere because of interest or desire, our beings, in an essential way, will be present there. Clairvoyant people will be able to be aware of our astral aspect and by focusing on it they can imaginatively elucidate who we are, describe our appearance and activity and even communicate or interact with what is often an unconscious aspect of us.

Many of the apparitions people see are people in curiosity exploring them or their homes astrally, or etheric remnants of people who were there before or are etherically connected now. At times we may have images of people in their home settings as our attention may be with them astrally without us realizing.

According to how we perceive, there will be a different level of clarity or accuracy. We can be: feeling people spiritually within us; looking at an image that has been sent to us; seeing the image of a person that they are carrying with them as they visit us astrally; remembering them from the past; spiritually perceiving them in their physical body now; or seeing an auric aspect of them. Our other spiritual senses can be operating at these different levels as well. The accuracy of our spiritual perception depends on how we are perceiving and if we know this we can relate to our perceptions or what we receive appropriately.

Some people are able to bring conscious attention to their astral bodies so that instead of receiving impressions that arise after being out astrally, they are able to be fully conscious at a distant time or place at will.

With our astral aspects we can explore realms of shared concepts, imagination, or patterns and perhaps other realms that humans are rarely involved in. Our astral bodies can be out at any time but most of our astral activity occurs when the needs of our other bodies are met. When we are asleep, engaged in simple or repetitive tasks, such as driving or routine work, we can be very active astrally according to our desires, thoughts and fantasies of the moment or that we were unable to complete earlier. Whenever our etheric body is able to maintain us, without further direction, we can be free to explore through other realms.

In groups where we are all being still together or

following a ritual or routine, or sharing a common focus, then our physical bodies and activities can be organized by the group and our spiritual bodies can be in spiritual realms together, following an agenda of our own or of the group.

In meditation we bring our physical and etheric bodies to a state of temporary completion, so that with consciousness we can bring our attention anywhere we choose.

However, during much of our life, our physical needs can require us to be task oriented. The work we have to do, the needs our physical bodies have, or the physical requirements of our lives, may organize all of our different levels for us. Our attention may not go to other levels and we may rarely think, feel or want except in relation to our tasks. Our astral and etheric bodies will still be active but mainly in relation to what we have been focusing our attention on.

People can be ruled by different bodies, and this is usually the basis of their temperaments, or they can consider them all and act from their selves co-operating with their community.

With our feelings we can weigh up all the forces at work, whether our own or from elsewhere and feel out the most suitable response or we can use thought to explore consciously. With our will we can overcome any unwanted forces or impose our own. When our physical body is healthy we can easily carry out our decisions.

It is only from our selves or our egos that we are able to act in consciousness. When our other bodies are dominant we may never understand what is driving us or choose where we are heading for. We can be organized intuitively by our perceived physical needs, our past desires or conditioning, or our communities without ever realizing.

When our thoughts, feelings and will are in harmony we can be powerful in the world with our choices of the moment flowing through easily as we choose them.

Someone who is fully conscious can become aware of what they receive immediately and choose what to allow to affect their beliefs, goals and actions. The intuitions or impulses, dreams and images, insights or inspirations that arise in us can flow directly into physical expressions or we can consider them further in consciousness and respond through spiritual realms instead.

When our spiritual foundations have been well built, we can act intuitively in the world with confidence. Otherwise we may need to accept the guidance and forces of our leaders and others focused on us. As we alter our foundations we also alter what we create spiritually or express physically. People with strong personal foundations can flow with other people at any level and influence them. If they have chosen their purpose, goals and parameters with consideration of their community, the intuitive influence they create can be of benefit to everyone.

22 The relationship of our spiritual bodies to each other.

Our etheric nature saturates all of our physical body as well as being interconnected with our astral body and community. It can affect the life-energy of a place and interact with the electromagnetic energy of the physical ingredients there. To some extent it can also interact with and organize the physical activities of people present.

Where our astral body can inspire events or coordinate them, through our etheric body we can will them directly or leave patterns from which events can unfold. With every expiration or perspiration we leave some of our essence behind with the place or object. We also leave some of our essential nature that we can remain connected to.

Our astral and etheric bodies are connected so that there is a flow between them and they check or balance each other. Our desire body is expansive, taking us out into the world to explore or organize new possibilities with people astrally, while our etheric body forms and limits changes, and protects us, and other people, from chaotic change.

Our astral body can go out with a single impulse without any organization so that decisions in the moment are difficult astrally, and curious people may simply observe with no involvement. When some of our etheric nature is present with us astrally our training can begin to act and we can deal automatically with whatever we perceive, If a person is able to be fully conscious while present spiritually they would be able to make considered responses to what they perceive.

Our " I " can at any time alter the activities of our etheric and astral bodies which could otherwise continue according to past directions until the forces motivating them are redirected or completed. Through the activities of the astral and etheric bodies our " I " directs the activities of our physical bodies as well. In mindfulness this could be each moment or it could be through the choices we constantly make that set patterns for the future.

In our exploration of the world our " I " or ego, creates new desires which, in a healthy person, must first flow through to the etheric body to be checked against personal conditioning before being acted upon.

Our physical body in all of its activities trains us to perform further any skills it is engaged in. The forms involved in this training flow through to organize other areas of our lives and the forces created can flow through to habits, attitudes, desires and ways of thinking.

While our ego can direct from one end and make changes in our spiritual bodies, our physical activities can affect our spiritual bodies from the other end. At the same time, through the interflow between people, there are constant changes to our etheric and astral bodies. These require us to be continually adjusting or reconciling ourselves to the changes at different levels.

Much of modern life is physical body based, with less of our training a result of communion with others or nature, or through rituals, ceremonies, stories, myths and legends which all use other more imaginative or intuitive aspects of our beings. It is as if our physical life, including our sports, computer games and work, is often dominating our spiritual life rather than the reverse.

With any new physical activity we could do it endlessly until we have created the appropriate patterns to follow in future, as in sports, crafts or skills, or we could think it through, do visualizations of how it needs to be, and empower our desires after relaxing. By using all these levels we can learn physical skills with very little practise.

If a persons desire nature is too powerful, or disorganized because of conflicting desires, to be directed by his ego or conditioned body then he will be chaotic in his own impulses and vulnerable to what he receives through his groupsoul, or from powerful individuals. He could be easily inspired or suggestible beyond his level of discernment. Alternatively his desires may organize him and his community through his being able to act without constraint.

If our conditioning body is too strong we may not be able to overcome our conditioning. Our habits, obsessions, addictions, beliefs, routines may all bind us so that even if there are valuable new possibilities available and we can recognize them, we may not be able to accept them. Our conditioning body is the basis of our will and if it has been well formed we can be very powerful through it.

Getting to know our selves and healing our ego, in its relationship with our other bodies and our community, enables us to act in the world in an effective and balanced way. We can ensure that our conditioned patterns and our desires are effective while still being open to change whenever we use our ego to choose again. Our conscious selves can become the director of our lives as a result.

23 *Altering our spiritual bodies.*

Our soul nature was evident at birth and has been developed further with our every experience so that to change our astral and etheric bodies is usually slow, except through initiations, religious conversions or traumas. It may be easier and more fruitful to redirect personal forces and to work with our own nature, instead of against it.

Much that we are, is interconnected to many of our other qualities so that change to some aspects may require many adjustments elsewhere, which we may not want. The imbalances we each have enable diversity between people and make up our personality. Nevertheless life moves on and changes may be needed to help us act in the world effectively, or to come to harmony within ourselves and with other people.

By adjusting to experiences, whether physical or spiritual, consciously or intuitively, we change ourselves and our own spiritual bodies. We can wait for events to arise which force us to adapt or we can evoke issues to explore, imagine new possibilities or create a space in which we can actively review old or foundation areas of our lives. By always responding to what arises our changes may only be peripheral ones whereas by going to the core of our beings and choosing again, we can affect many areas of our lives at once.

Having foundations in place, that we have personally chosen or created, enables us to trust our intuitive responses, freeing us to explore new areas of desire or interest. With each new experience we are able to bring new ingredients under the direction of our desire or conditioned body and reorganize or let go of old ones. As a result our conscious attention can be free to be actively engaged in any area, living in each moment.

The forces we have created in the past need to be completed and we can do this spiritually or through physical experiences. By exploring possibilities spiritually we can let go of old possibilities without needing physical events to experience and explore them. Any new forces we create with our thoughts and desires will affect people spiritually and often lead to new physical events to complete them or bring them to consciousness. Through our mind activities we alter our karmas.

With thought we can create and evoke desires and feelings, self images and imaginings or memories which we can alter, clear or empower so that we make changes to our desire body. Our desires, emotions and goals can be affected as a result of clearing the mental ingredients that support them. These changes can in turn flow through to our habitual body, altering abilities, life-energy flows, beliefs, routines and intuitive responses and in turn flow to our physical body to be expressed as changes in health, physical appearance, skills or behavioral activity.

Someone who thinks constantly and with clarity can be continually developing their own spiritual bodies and in turn directing their community through their own changes. When a person's thoughts are suitable they will influence others and be accepted but when they are inconsiderate of the community, they may be rejected or limited.

Acting from our higher selves helps us ensure that our community can participate in whatever we try to create. By allowing our h.selves to feel out situations or people we open up to sources other than our own desire and conditioned bodies. We can still choose what to be influenced by but we have the opportunity to attempt to transcend any conflicts with our own positions so that our beings can remain in harmony with our community.

How we behave astrally depends on how we have created and trained our desires and emotions in our everyday life. Often our astral behaviour will be quite different from our physical responses because we may never express much of what we want or think and empower our astral body instead.

We can receive feelings, dreams and insights, and unconscious transfers, or learn each moment from our physical interactions, so that our image of ourselves, of other people and of our involvement in the world is constantly changing.

If there is inadequate communication on a conscious level more of it will occur between people unconsciously. If agendas are different everyone may be battling for influence with little scope for conscious assessment.

There is a process of integration and reconciliation of all new experiences and insights, that we receive at any level or from any person, with our old positions. There is also an ongoing attempt to keep our different bodies in harmony with each other and any conflicts we have can be expressed in our thoughts, self image, desires, behaviour or physical health. Observing any imbalance at any level we can take action to loosen up or strengthen ourselves when necessary.

The process of change needs to avoid direct confrontations as these are exhausting. It helps to choose areas that are worth changing so that we can be enthusiastic about the process. If we first let go of our negativities, fears and aversions, we can create something new that is supported, rather than in conflict with other aspects of ourselves.

If our different bodies are in harmony with each other the process of reconciliation can cease so that we can relax and be at one with our selves. In this state we are free to dedicate all of our life-energy to new creativity or supporting others, enabling ourselves to be more effective in the world.

With every thought we have there can be a flow through to our astral and etheric bodies to alter them. This process requires life-energy both to overcome the existing positions and to fix the new ones in place so that it can tire us. If our desire and conditioning bodies are well organized they can accommodate new thoughts easily and our changes in the world can flow through naturally. If a change is too difficult for us we may experience blockages to change in our thoughts, attitudes, desires, habits and to our life-energy flows and affecting our muscles and organs as well.

We can be ruthless about personal changes or we can accept our humanity and only alter the necessary areas that are blocking us. By making changes, or having mini rebirths, each day we are able to constantly change in a balanced way.

By changing harmoniously we allow people we are connected to keep up with our changes. Due to our inter-connections it becomes necessary to inspire possibilities for people we are connected to, to change harmoniously to, or at least to expand to allow our changes.

24 Our etheric body and health.

While our etheric, or conditioning, body supports and directs our physical activities through every cell, it also directs the systemic changes to our physical body through our meridians, and directs the flow to and from our astral body and other people through our chakras.

Our flow of life-energy reflects our own physical, emotional and mental states. It also reflects our relationship to the world and other people. Areas where the flow is congested or depleted can be detected by masseurs, acupuncturists and energy balancers or anyone who has trained themselves to focus on life-energy flows intimately.

Any imbalances to the energy flow will eventually show up in muscular, organ and system imbalances. Often, even before we feel the discomforts in different parts of our physical body, we may observe related changes in our attitudes to ourselves or others, or feel the change of attitude towards us from other people.

Temporary attitude changes are often the result or cause of an imbalance of energy so that feelings of guilt, jealousy, prejudice, loss of faith, self reproach, arrogance, obsession or numerous others, are often indications that personal challenge needs to be met, let go or supported. As a temporary measure, to give us a rest from the problems caused by the imbalance, our chakras could be balanced by a therapist or directly by ourselves, if we know how.

Sometimes, as soon as we accept a new role or image of ourselves, or others, the health or attitudinal problem we have had, disappears.

In all of our relationship imbalances we can come to ask whether it is the issue, a need for support of some kind by us or others, or a temporary imbalance that we, or the other person, needs to explore. Knowing there are many causes of conflict, we can detach from them and take them less personally.

Due to the precise nature of our energy imbalances it is possible for trained practitioners to identify likely areas we need to deal with in our relationships, attitudes or self image from the physical indications or the areas of energy imbalance. While they can clear congested areas or enliven depleted areas by moving the energy along or out giving temporary relief, permanent changes may require us to change in corresponding areas of our lives as well.

There are precise correspondences on many levels of our lives due to the inter-connections of our own spiritual bodies and with the spiritual bodies of our associates. There are also correspondences between our needs and essential aromas, colors, sounds, herbs, times of moon and year, and homeopathic remedies so that when a person is ill there is a range of temporary courses of action to take. Most of the remedies listed above operate by evoking resonance in the etheric body, stimulating it to restore itself.

We can also assist the strengthening of our etheric body by using particular formed or repetitive movements or set appropriate habits and routines. Repeating appropriate mantras or joining in group chanting can also be very healing for the etheric body and the group. With a healthy etheric body, health at all levels is more likely as a result.

While we can heal the etheric body directly, we can also affect it through its links to our physical and astral bodies and ego. We can deal with imbalances in it through diets and chosen exercises with the physical body or through visualizations with our astral body or by thinking through any conflicts or challenges. As all of our bodies are connected a change in one will attempt to flow through to the other bodies. Where we make the changes could depend on where the problem is or what we are capable of. There is a range of creative and meditational activities which stimulate changes at these spiritual levels which eventually flow through to our etheric body.

In theory we could all learn to heal ourselves or keep ourselves in balance by learning to focus our attention on any balanced range of objects, moods, colors, tones, tastes, movements, people, or activities in a similar way to balancing any surplus or deficit in our food diet. If all of our senses are awakened and well nurtured then we automatically seek to participate in life in a balanced way.

Poor health can be overcome by removing blockages to natural health as easily as by providing additional substances or disciplines.

In trying to balance ourselves we can choose from a range of different levels of activities or experiences according to our personal preferences as many of them correspond to each other. We could be out of balance in a color but use particular sounds or foods to balance us instead. Each person can find their own methods, that suit them, to enable them to come to balance and health in their life.

While we are all responsible for our own health and need to choose it actively, many of our imbalances originate through our intuitive interactions with other people. We may notice in ourselves after being with particular individuals, groups or places that we are off balance in our moods, thoughts, desires, attitudes, even down to getting pain in different parts of our bodies immediately with some people. This could be due to their individual patterns or with the attitudes, aromas, colors, tones, activities or speeds that they participate in, that suit them, but not us at that moment.

All the imbalances that result from a conflict between us and others intuitively, can be disowned. All etheric imbalances can be temporary and we can let them go. We can also get hooked on them if they stimulate an issue of our own that we have yet to complete or balance.

Taking on particular fears, aversions, or attitudes which are inappropriate can lead to ill health at other levels too. We have an option whether to accept them or let them go. Accepting imbalances, perhaps in self sacrifice, enables us to explore an issue and try to resolve it for our community and in the process we can strengthen ourselves.

The actual dynamic of individual health and even morality, is a group one, so that our well-being, states of mind, self image, as well as our life and financial successes are created through the dynamic spiritual interactions between ourselves and other people. If we feel ourselves being diminished, particularly during our life transitions when many of our parameters and goals have loosened up, it is important that we assert the image of ourselves that we prefer and ensure that the attitudes we impose on others are useful ones. We all can choose health in ourselves while enabling others to do so as well.

25 The flow of spiritual forces between people.

As our consciousness grows it becomes possible to interact with people completely through spiritual realms. We can respond to what they communicate to us spiritually or from what we observe of them spiritually.

As each thought, reaction or desire, that relates to us, occurs in another person, it can flow through to us, so that we can be aware of it as if present with them. If we wish we can let the forces flow past with detachment or we can respond as we choose.

The flow of spiritual forces between people is the basis of spiritual guidance, spiritual healing, and cooperative creation of the future and it contributes to the cultural evolution of a community. This flow can be conscious in some individuals and is active intuitively through the rest of the community.

When there is no consciousness of what is occurring in other realms then the forces we impose on others will be without any conscious consideration of them. Our spiritual activity will be from our goals and parameters, result from what we perceive of them physically in a brief incident, or be intuitive or trained responses, to what we receive from them spiritually. None of these responses will be truly considerate of the other people.

There is a flow between people constantly at a habitual level which can create in us unsolicited changes that we can accept or deal with when they arise to consciousness.

This flow can happen whenever we intuitively focus on each other, or occur naturally whenever we are together physically.

The intuitive flow between us is often directed by our conversations or actions, but it can also be a result of what we have prepared in our thoughts in the past that relate to the other person, or be from our own agendas and training, which can flow through at an etheric level more easily when we are together. Often the content of our unconscious transfers is completely different to our conscious ones. Some people who hardly speak when in company, or share inconsequential matters that they needn't give much attention to, may be sharing a lot on an intuitive level and may be using the mutual focus through the conversation to make the flow easier.

How we perceive people affects how we relate to them spiritually or physically and many waves can be created between us if we are out of harmony, with each person reacting. These intuitive reactions can escalate, leading to exhaustion, loss of sleep or disturbances in both of us.

Bringing our consciousness to the flow can bring an end to the sequence of automatic reactions. Sometimes a third person, who is spiritually able, can step in to resolve the conflict as if there is an imbalance in any individual it can easily spread and affect the whole community.

We are able to share our forces at different levels directly. We can share thoughts using telepathy, with words, concepts, images or prepared visualizations or we can share with our feelings or dreams. We can also share with our will, intuitively flowing the essence of what we are about, whether we have first thought it out, or visualized it, or just know what we want. In a more direct way we can alter the chakras of other people with our own, changing their speeds or redirecting the nature or types of desires they have.

Our chakras are being constantly adjusted by more powerful people so that when we join a community we are assisted to more easily share attitudes, philosophies, goals and timing with others. When we make our own choices and resist the flow of community life we may also affect our chakras taking them out of alignment with people or impose something new from our forces on our community.

While we may be acting from thought the effects we have on others may be at any level according to who they are. With our thoughts we can affect people at different levels so that they can be assisted in consciousness with verbal suggestions they recognize as ours or have insights where whole concepts are received as a package and can then be gradually unfolded by them. They could feel out new impulses, images, emotions and desires, or have intuitive knowledge, as a result of our involvement with them.

By sending suitable images we can inspire changes in people which can affect them consciously or through dreams or intuitively so that their motivation is changed. By being strong in ourselves we affect patterns of behaviour directly and may even flow directly into their physical actions of the moment on an intuitive level without intending to or realizing it ourselves. There are many ethical issues here about spiritual trespass, but people have been praying or wishing for each other for a long time so it is quite normal and it may be more important to learn how to deal with it.

Some people may be conscious spiritually but have little concern or even mindfulness of their physical actions so that they often accept the impulses of other people. They may assume their acceptance will lead to harmony with others, even if they have no clear picture or idea about what is happening or why they are acting as they are.

If the sharing of minds is intuitive it may not flow through to a physical level until events cause us to act from it, and it is as if what we have learnt spiritually can then come into being.

Anything that we can perceive, recall or create with our minds can be shared spiritually. This can all be harmonious whether we are conscious of it or not and if there is conflict it will eventually come to consciousness for us to explore or resolve. What we receive can enable us to expand or come to clarity in any area of our lives affected by it.

On a spiritual level we may have accepted, for many different reasons, to co-operate in events that we never would do if asked directly. Our supraconsciousness is much greater than our awareness of the moment and what can appear threatening to us when seen at a glimpse can be very advantageous when having a broader view.

Knowing ourselves we can trust our intuition even if we have to struggle through the events we get involved in. If we have accepted new patterns inappropriately, situations will arise to explore them, so that we can in consciousness alter them again if we wish to.

Some of the training we receive spiritually from people relates almost exclusively to spiritual realms. In a society where many people do not believe in man's spiritual nature, people can be precisely accurate in their spiritual activities while still preventing their own involvement from coming to consciousness. Most successful people are powerful or wise spiritually, whether they know it or not.

There are shared patterns that are developed over centuries in a nation of people, which can remain long after the society they were created in and for, is over. There may have been a collapse of a civilisation, after which the opportunities for expressing the patterns is lost. They can remain as a part of the people and be passed on intuitively until a new renaissance is possible. Events may arise again, where the patterns are relevant once more, and people's intuitive abilities will enable them to perform new, but related, tasks or understand new concepts easily.

As a result of this disparity between people's spiritual patterning or potential and the actual expression in the physical realm, there is often a considerable difference between who people are in the physical world and who they are in spiritual realms. A child at birth may already have available much that they require spiritually but need the opportunities for this to come to consciousness or to be expressed in physical activities. Compared to the complete picture of who we are as spirits, our life on the physical level of reality may only add a little to our spiritual potential.

Our spiritual activity directed at other people can be direct from our thoughts or first flow more deeply into our own desire or conditioned bodies so that we interact with people from these. This interaction could be conscious if we can bring our consciousness to our astral activity or it could be intuitive once we had created the necessary forces in our conditioning bodies.

If we relate to people from our hearts we can avoid getting involved in detailed suggestions or manipulations allowing a range of sources, including our own, to guide us, giving greater opportunity for harmony. Our hearts are broad-ranging, intuitively considering everything whereas in our thoughts we can become very narrow, or base decisions on a narrow view of the world.

When we have strong foundations that are well organized we can continue to have an affect on everyone we think of or come into contact with without needing to give the interflow any conscious consideration. Our wills will interact whenever possible to change the world to our personal positions through altering the positions and directions of other people intuitively. This can be a road to power but rarely a road to wisdom or harmony.

Through our heart connections we can accept others and allow them to relax. We can both expand in bounteousness to accommodate each other in sufficient ways for harmony to be possible. With our heads we are often forcing people to come to consciousness in areas they may not be ready for, tiring them. With our wills we may attempt to dominate which can also be exhausting or diminishing.

Through confidence and the belief in a timely unfolding of the world we can allow people to take their time and allow them to accept opportunities as they arise rather than impose changes on them. Through our feelings we can be easily influenced by others but with confidence we can know that we are able to choose anew each moment of our life and that no influence is absolute or permanent. In times of transition we may need to be assertive because the intuitive harmony has been disturbed, but once harmony is possible we can change our mode of relating again, rather than habitually imposing on others to protect ourselves.

The cost of a strong will is that we may have difficulty in being flexible. While we can dominate others through it, it may prevent us appreciating life in new ways and we may adopt attitudes that allow us to be dominant rather than open to others.

Even on a spiritual level there can be many unexpected conflicts as the people we meet or call up may have been trained or have an image of themselves as a helper and will try to help, even if this is not what we want. Each person intuitively responds from who they are and how they perceive the situation, as well as what we have asked for. Knowing this we can learn to accept the best and ignore the rest.

As much of what occurs between people psychically is due to our unconscious forces, it is possible to create great attraction or psychic warfare without intending to. When we discover these sources of conflicts with people we can become more forgiving, realizing our humanity in the process.

The different methods and pathways for influence and empowerment that are used between people depend on the temperaments of the people involved. As a result there are also different levels of consciousness in all spiritual interactions, both within the person who is creating the influence and in the person or group they are influencing.

There are also different methods of bringing spiritual perceptions to consciousness. If we are affected through our conditioned body we may need to imaginatively recreate the forces involved from what we receive intuitively whereas if we perceive astrally we can see directly the activity that is occurring and a higher level of accuracy is usually possible. People may notice the changes in themselves as they participate in experiences in new ways.

Any thought, image or concept we receive can evoke a range of different responses in us so that we make use of what we receive in a personalized way. Our unconscious forces can participate in the development of anything we receive to present it to our consciousness in a personally meaningful way. Alternatively we can allow the forces to flow through to a will level so that we will automatically fit into events, knowing what, how and when to act.

When I receive telepathically or intuitively from people it is often difficult to know for certain whether I am receiving from a conscious or intuitive aspect of them. Most of what we all share flows intuitively without our knowledge and unfortunately this can be a source of confusion. What we receive can be central to their life's purpose or trivia of the moment so we need to be discerning about it.

Any change in ourselves creates change in our connections or change through our connections without needing any conscious awareness of the other people or the process. There are many habitual patterns available to enable all of these changes to occur smoothly to avoid having to consciously give them attention.

We could keep our communication or interaction completely on the physical level, without thinking, feeling or wanting anything in response so that the moment it was over the person or experience could be forgotten. Alternatively the effects of the physical event may continue for a while with each person contributing and reacting further, generating new thoughts, desires, emotions as well as releasing or expressing old ones.

There is a feedback system which we can eventually share with our minds or through our actions. If we deal with all spiritual forces, leading to new experiences or possible conflicts, on a spiritual level we will no longer need to be part of the physical events to learn from or complete them.

Spiritual interactions could continue on and off for years after a physical one, each time they return to mind. Spiritual imbalances create karmic forces which attempt to bring us together in a new physical event in order to resolve the imbalance. This can be with the same or with different people.

If we become conscious in spiritual realms, or take notice of indicators of imbalance in our dreams or events of the day, it becomes possible to resolve spiritual conflicts without needing physical events to occur. The two people would both change or expand to transcend the conflict, with the extent of the change being affected by the depth of the conflict or the depth of longing for the change.

How we deal with and respond to what happens during any of the flows, influences people so that through the flows we sort each other out, winning and losing friends as we go. We can be misled by the forces at work on us or we can receive each experience with equanimity taking the best from it and creating something positive. We can respond habitually or use consideration each time. As we change ourselves, and our intuitive responses, we change our relationship with the world and to some extent, the world itself.

By focusing our attention in positive thoughts and images powerfully before sleeping and all day if we are able, we enable ourselves to be effective in our unconscious journeys, and to avoid many possible conflicts.

CHAPTER FIVE

THE FLOW OF

LIFE-ENERGY.

When we have an abundance of life-energy, we can learn or train ourselves very easily, can have and empower many new possibilities and will have easy success in bringing about our, or our communities, desires.

All spiritual activity requires us to provide life-energy to it, to bring about the change, but in cases where the change leads to a letting go, additional life energy will become available once we do so.

26 *The flow of life-energy between our spiritual bodies.*

When we have an abundance of life-energy, we can learn or train ourselves very easily, can have and empower many new possibilities and will have easy success in bringing about our desires. This abundance can be made available by ourselves in health and relaxation and from our community supporting us. At other times we can set our priorities precisely so that the life-energy we have available is dedicated to it so that we can be successful in that area.

During stressful times our life-energy goes into our physical activities, astral preparations or training so that our health can suffer as a result. If the stress continues for long enough our capacity to remember, maintain habits and routines, and our ability to have new aspirations, will be sacrificed. Our conditioning body will reorganize itself, letting go of the inessentials, to provide additional life-energy. At times long held abilities, such as driving a car, may be lost and will have to be relearned. In the extremes, as in some kinds of initiation or trauma people may completely forget their childhood language as the spiritual body which enabled it can be disempowered too far.

All spiritual activity requires us to provide life-energy to it, to bring about the change, but in cases where the change leads to a letting go, additional life energy will become available once we do so.

Understanding the process of energy flow we can have a quiet time of relaxation or meditation before attempting to learn or visualizing new possibilities.

When with someone who needs to learn, we can ensure that we are not taking the energy they need by relaxing and support them instead. There are techniques for attracting energy and directing it to people precisely to support them, but this can be a nuisance when performed inappropriately by beginners.

According to where we dedicate most of our energy we will influence our temperament and our way of relating to the world. Firstly we can focus on physical needs and tasks. Secondly we can dedicate our energy to training ourselves and set our parameters out of enjoyment, in competition or through fear of failure, taking in life-energy and increasing our will power by doing so. Thirdly in confidence we can explore new possibilities or events, imagine and plant the seeds that create the patterns for ourselves and others to fit in with to bring them about, and we can use our energy to empower these. We may give little thought to training or self protection. Fourthly, we can increase the energy we always have available so that increasing our consciousness of the moment, and act with discernment and consideration in all that we are a part of.

There is a flow of life-energy through and between our different spiritual bodies constantly as we alter or develop our physical and spiritual bodies further. At each level we can interact with other people, spiritually, verbally, astrally, etherically or through our physical behaviour and appearance, or we can take the life-energy to other levels to be expressed or interact in a different way.

By always speaking or expressing our thoughts and feelings we may diminish the intensity of our desires or training. By remaining silent we can become powerful or disturbed in our emotions and effect people and events strongly through spiritual realms.

We can direct our own life-energy in different ways. We can have thoughts and express them in speech, without remembering them, or we can take them into ourselves into images of possibilities and desires. By visualizing we can train ourselves to prepare both the events and our own activities in them. By rehearsing, or training our bodies we can prepare our physical body so that it is best suited for the roles we imagine for ourselves. The images we or other people have of us, and our lives, help to form our physical bodies, intuitively co-ordinating our diets and interest in exercise or activities in preparation.

Each person expresses themselves in their own way according to the bodies that they are most comfortable with. As a result some people can be powerful astrally with little consciousness or ability in the physical world, or conscious with little astral or etheric activity.

People organize or empower their spiritual bodies according to their own particular needs, interests or fears. Some people may over empower their conditioned bodies, in an attempt at controlling their worlds, to the point of limiting their ability to change. They may be unable to act against habitual responses, or see other people doing so, without suffering distress. Other people may empower their desires far beyond their personal capacities to fulfill them. We can get indications of where people act from by observing their behaviour.

Knowing our own imbalances we can come to choose to disempower or redirect them enabling us to come to freedom in ourselves. There are many meditational practices which enable us to take in or release our energy at will or that assist us to let go of inappropriate conditioning, self images and desires, giving us the energy we need.

People who observe themselves can discover activities naturally that help them focus or relax as they need to. There may be a kind of changing of gears as we start work each day or as we arrive home that enables the change.

If we are finding that our life-energy doesn't go far enough, rather than playing power games or disempowering others we can give ourselves a rest each day or reduce our desires or our needs for training and find some life enhancing activities instead. If our lives become more demanding we may need to give greater consideration to looking after our spiritual needs.

27 Sharing out life-energy amongst people.

We subtly influence each other constantly through our connections but we also empower each other, particularly in times of need. This could be from our surplus of life-force. It could also be in self sacrifice, and at great cost, if we feel someone is worth supporting or if we are habitually open to them and they draw in powerfully. By sharing we can ensure that everyone in our community has enough in their times of need and we can all benefit as a result.

Our etheric body is involved in organizing the habitual flow of energy with people we are connected to according to the relationships we have with them. With our astral body we will be trying to empower future events and anyone who can contribute to them.

These flows of support can be equal and mutual but occur at different times so that in a healthy community the flows can all balance out. If a relationship is permanently out of balance a person may involuntarily and habitually be supporting and empowering the people they are connected to at a cost to their life-energy. Hopefully they would still benefit in other ways as a result of being part of the group.

Some people are very lighthearted and trusting and are happy to support everyone else as they have few wants of their own. Other people need to be in control of everything and will draw to themselves the necessary life-energy to be so.

While we can have particular energy needs how much we will draw, or allow ourselves to accept, may depend on our own self image or self esteem. Our beliefs about ourselves may need to change before we alter the flow between ourselves and others so that we have sufficient for our own needs. To this end many people with desires greater than their personal ability to realize, create an image of themselves that will create a flow of support to them. They may continually redefine themselves to allow themselves to take a greater share of the communal pool of life-energy.

In being afraid of someone, seeing ourselves as inferior or less worthy, or supporting them excessively due to a false image of them, we can empower them to our cost. By bringing our relationships to balance with people the intuitive flow with them will also be balanced.

Any person in a community who is regarded as valuable gains more support than average. In this way a community ensures that the best influences are empowered while others, and the people with them, are not. People who have needs for additional support may spend a lot of time and effort convincing people they are worth it. There are many games played to establish a persons rights to a greater share.

If I have a surplus of life-energy I can flow out to influence others. If my cup is full and I am complete in all areas I won't accept new influences or possibilities. If someone wishes to be intuitively influential they may first upset or dominate a person, opening them up to influence.

Life-energy is usually flavored with a persons agenda or parameters so that to receive energy from others means that we will be influenced unless we transform the contents. It can happen that when people feel they are supporting others, in meditation or prayer, they may be creating exhausting conflicts instead. At times, all of us have a surplus and what creates conflict in one person will not in someone who can deal with it. Through the circulation of new possibilities, attitudes and desires, our society can continue to spiritually evolve.

If while relaxing or meditating we happen to focus on someone else we may instantly feel a change of energy, a release or arrival of energy right down to a muscular level. Our agitation may go or our exhaustion may be over or we may suddenly feel much worse. For this reason it is beneficial to be able to keep our attention where we choose to so that we don't give people unnecessary burdens or drain them in inappropriate energy transfers.

Many people are reluctant to accept or share other peoples energy unless fully focused in a task where they transform any influence to their own needs immediately. They usually ensure that they retain a higher level of training or greater intentions and the level of tension in their physical bodies is usually higher as a result. These people may fear their times of recreation if they stop being focused, as the types of thoughts, feelings and impulses that can arise can create agitation or confusion in them. Other people may have learnt to dismiss unusual thoughts or impulses, simply choosing the best of what arises.

Leaders, with the surplus life-energy from their community support, can have enormous personal power to use to direct their community, while other individuals may struggle to have any thoughts or desires of their own.

It is possible to come to be able to choose the flow of life-energy to or from us so that spiritual leaders with many supporters can draw and direct life-force as they wish or find a natural source of life-energy so that they can be fountains of support for their communities.

For most people the source of non human life-energy is their food or their involvement with nature. It is possible to consciously obtain energy directly from the sun, or air or other elements, but this is rare beyond our own individual needs, as humans are not sufficiently evolved to do this easily. Some people do it for short periods but the process of large scale energy flows can unbalance them. When we know how to draw or accept or convert this life-force we may have an almost unlimited supply, and the life-energy can be circulated through a community with some people making more use of it than others. In this way it may one day become possible for people to abandon their competition for life-energy.

The easiest way for everyone to have enough would be for us all to reduce our desires, unless part of a group agenda, to what we can personally achieve, and to co-operate so that we needn't train or protect ourselves as much.

28 Negotiating the flows of life-energy.

Most of what we do in our lives is organized by our conditioning body so that much that flows between people follows habitual pathways. What we establish in our conscious activities with people creates the patterns that we will follow intuitively at other times.

Many of our relationships were established earlier in our lives and they may not have been reviewed so that the habitual flows may still be continuing according to old agreements. This is the case with members of our family, past teachers and employers or even leaders in the army years earlier. Intuitively we may still respond to them all in spiritual realms, or in our spiritual activities, in the same old, way even though we have grown and their influence or role may no longer be relevant.

While we can have habitual relationships with particular people we can also have habitual ways of relating with everyone. This can be a result of our own nature or due to a role we may have worked or lived in for a long time.

Through the creation of a habitual relationship we also may create or accept expectations and obligations that intuitively organize our support or subservience whenever called for. Once established, these patterns of flow of empowerment may continue until there is an event which forces a change.

As we alter our agreements with other people we affect the route of life-energy support through our community and the flow of influence. We may be supported by new people and in support direct our attention differently. As a result some individuals increase their abilities to influence their communities while other people may be diminished in this.

Agreements about habitual support have nothing to do with fairness or justice. Some people will organize dominance in every interaction with other people so that they can always choose the direction of the flow, whereas others will be supporters or victims, not understanding why they usually feel powerless.

A man going to work on behalf of his family or community may expect to receive or take life-energy in order to be able to achieve his goals. The family may feel obliged to support him in all of his activities as they share in the benefits he gains. At other times the husband may support the family but the flow amongst members of a family is often uneven. Somehow, after negotiation, a workable balance is reached where energy is distributed in a workable way.

Particularly while focused in work, we can draw energy strongly from anyone who supports us. When we create a vacuum for energy by engaging in a task powerfully, or pushing ourselves to the limit, we pull energy in from where ever it is available, aspects of our selves, people we are connected to or those who have an interest in our project.

Physical activity itself doesn't usually require additional life-energy and often it enables our own energy to flow more effectively. However when we use our wills in pushing ourselves to greater effort or if we need to think to organize our activity, or if we empower our desires to bring them about, we may need far more life-energy than we have available. Working hard in habitual ways can be relaxing for everyone but the additional needs can require us to seek life-energy support from other people.

Traditionally a wife supported her husband so that there were many social expectations that needed to be reviewed when women began to work away from home.

Wives may have needed to find new ways to gain support as well as ways of feeling comfortable about giving their children less attention.

The normal routes of support in a family could have been from the relaxing father through the wife to the children. While he worked the wife supported him from home, either with her energy or by acting as his muse, assisting him with her thoughts and prayers in all he did.

The expected roles and relationships and even attitudes were organized to enable this to occur smoothly. As wives began to play a dynamic role and had to assert themselves to meet new challenges outside of the home, a whole new pattern of habitual and predictable flow of energy has needed to be developed within the family and throughout the community.

Whenever there is a change new arrangements need to be made that will affect everyone. If someone starts or stops working, becomes ill or grows up, joins or leaves the groupsoul, reductions or additional burdens are made. If the change is a predictable one there can be a gradual adjustment before the change but with traumatic changes of deaths, retrenchment in jobs or divorce, the adjustment is after the event and is attempted in a time of confusion.

People can receive a lot of support due to a public position or role to enable their tasks. Their personal friends and family may be supported from the surplus they receive but once they give up the role the energy flow through them can change dramatically. Other people may have accumulated a pool of energy through training or long term struggle so that once they relax they can support others for a long time until it is shared out.

Due to these changes in energy level upon relaxation some people avoid it altogether and may never allow themselves a holiday in case the effort to return to their former level of action is too great. Some people act from natural ability and a little effort and will be able to relax easily while others can be pushing themselves to perform better constantly and be fearful of relaxing.

Sometimes we attempt to cut off from people as a result of disappointment, feelings of abuse or inappropriate influence. We might do this spontaneously without having brought ourselves to balance first so that the imbalance can continue for years and lead to bitterness and isolation.

When we are out of balance in a relationship we will usually oscillate in our power flow, giving out until we feel the loss and then in annoyance or antagonism, attempt to reclaim it. By coming to balance we no longer need to support others inappropriately, no longer will come to a point of having too little or feeling it, and no longer need to organize other people to hand over their energy to us.

Everyone needs more support sometimes, in the moment, to train themselves or to empower their futures. People can all contribute at different times and in different ways so that leaders can be supported for the organization, protection or new possibilities they provide. The imbalances of any moment need to be seen in a broader context.

29 Effects of concentrating and relaxing

Within ourselves and then between ourselves and others the flow of energy changes as we concentrate or relax. If we focus powerfully we pull in our auras. As a result we change the influence and support we give those people around us. However if we pull in while they are focused on us, or we on them, then there will be a flow from them to us. If people pull in, through focusing their attention or in fear, this can be contagious with everyone doing the same to avoid being drained. If this is excessive some individuals may faint, be ill from it or be unable to think straight.

Children who are present with adults who are excessively focused in thought or debate, can feel disoriented from it and have accidents more easily or misbehave to redirect the flow to themselves, or to prevent themselves from being drained. They may also object to the negative or destructive flows of emotional scenes, feeling the distress in themselves.

Individuals who usually have a surplus of life-energy, or who have prepared themselves to be able to do so, can spread their auras over a whole crowd enabling everyone to feel the goodwill and to relax.

When a crowd listens to a speaker the mood can change rapidly according to whether excitement, anger or fear is being evoked and the energy will be constantly changing. This can also occur on a personal level as we can cause someone to drain us of energy, by evoking fear in them.

Being engaged in our interests, goals and parameters, means we will also be intuitively focused and interconnected as parts of us will be exploring, creating or limiting, and we can be less affected by the energy changes of the people around us. Without desires it is as if we are not making any use or claims on our own energy, so that it is more available to others. If we are part of a group that shares and protects our interests, this can be valuable, as the group will be able to act harmoniously rather than competitively. People will be able to act with confidence instead of from fear.

When two people are concentrating at once and they are open to each other there could be competition for the energy. When both are confident and focused in themselves, without focusing on the other person, any flow between them can be mutually supporting.

The competition for energy can be between individuals, groups or whole countries where the leaders may encourage everyone to train themselves as highly as possible, have an enormous range of desires and to compete in their work against people from foreign countries, as if they are about to be taken over.

When competition or fear of others is encouraged there will automatically be a shortage of life-energy which will be obvious in social chaos, stress, mental disturbances and ill health. People could be taught better ways of harnessing their energy and focusing their attention or instead the whole environment could be reorganized so that the system was improved and co-operation encouraged.

Most people can think more clearly and be more intuitive when relaxed than when competing with others. When there is competition or trauma there is polarization with the confident people being empowered and more brilliant than ever, and others unable to think for themselves.

When there is a surplus of life-energy in a group there can be a harmonious flow between the people so that activities can flow smoothly and little effort is required. By taking away unnecessary burdens, any group from families to large organizations, can become more harmonious.

Individuals can be encouraged to relax and start afresh rather than continually operate from outdated opposing conditioned positions. People who assume a harmony with each other are inclined to be mutually accepting and enable each other to feel empowered. People with naturally conflicting positions can exhaust each other despite their best intentions. Instead of accusing the other person of draining them, and creating further discomfort, it is helpful to transcend the causes of the conflict or focus elsewhere.

There are definite times of the day, week, and year when most people we know are focused on their tasks. Unless we are happy to support them this may not be a good time to be focused on them or to be over relaxed. If we find it difficult to focus, it can sometimes be easier when everyone else is relaxing. For this reason nights may be a good time for our energy for thinking or writing, even though our own physiology may prefer the mornings.

Our clarity of thought may be best when everyone is engaged on their own tasks and not focused on us. There are many different factors as the flow can be many ways at the same time and how we are affected could be determined by what we are engaged in or how strongly, as well as what other people we are connected to need.

Sometimes we may feel stress for no reason and try to relax and it may not improve. It could be more appropriate to focus on something that brings us in a little and prevent ourselves being drained, unless we know the cause and agree to support it. Our energy will also flow to where ever our attention is. By keeping our attention on suitable places we can choose suitable energy flows or interactions.

People who can concentrate easily are able to play with thoughts and can pull a whole range of them to them, and come up with new possibilities or combinations easily. Other people may not be able to concentrate and the process of exploring ideas may be almost impossible to them. As we concentrate we direct our available energy so that it is easier to remember anything we were focused on as well.

People who can harness the flow by concentrating are usually also in a position to influence their community because of the power of the flow through them. Other people may not be able to affect the flow through themselves at all, with thoughts not coming to consciousness much. With enthusiasm we are able to change gears in our energy levels which can make concentration much easier.

30 Games people play to get a greater share of the flow.

Whenever they feel it necessary, people will attempt to get other people to give them attention so that the life-energy will flow as they need it to. This could be with people they live with or they could go out to find what they need. This is a natural response we have which is similar to our need for a food supplement when our diet is off balance.

When people have too much life-energy they make seek opportunities to share it and at other times they may organize support. If necessary they may stir up a person's emotions to get the energy flowing so that changes in the flow are possible, enabling them to express something or take it in.

If we try to stop an habitual emotional game we will force a new variant to come into being unless the person's energy need has been addressed. When we discover ourselves playing games we can try to redirect them into more positive ones that everyone can benefit from.

People with a strong personal agenda, inconsiderate of group harmony, need to attract energy to them so they organize situations where they can be dominant and drawing.

When two people are relating they may be constantly attempting to subtly alter their energy relationships using all kinds of ploys. There may be attempts to establish permanent flows or temporary ones in times of need. A pecking order may be about who is dominant but the authority is one way and intuitive support is the other.

Different areas of life may be dwelt on in the negotiation stage so that the other person may be put in the right frame of mind. They may be inspired by a vision of a grand future to work towards together or guilt could be played with by reminding them of obligations, past mistakes or inconveniences. People may evoke an image of community praise for their good actions. Appeals to manhood, past contributions, virtues of charity or service or love of god may be mentioned. Promises may be made, of future reward, repayment, protection, guidance or flattery and praise may be given to invite reciprocal goodwill.

These games may all be played to alter the relationship to achieve particular ends and many people get very good at them. They may be designed to either get the other person off balance and vulnerable to dominance, or to ensure inadequate attention is given to the consequences. Sometimes they induce relaxation or excitement so that more energy is available and trust comes easily. People may have trained themselves so well that the whole game can continue without any consciousness of the purpose in any of them.

There are positive games that enable everyone to relax and cease having to waste life-energy defending themselves. Sharing a common dream and agreeing to mutual benefits, while ensuring that no one works too hard so that they have to rob others of their energy or try to, means that most of the trivial games will disappear, unless played for fun. Many games can be of benefit to everyone.

When everyone's needs are satisfied they can all relax and forget the interplays to gain their share. People who are satisfied with their lives may only play games that everyone can enjoy and benefit from.

When people assess what kind of person we are, they may intuitively attempt to evoke responses to gain support or influence. By acknowledging this intuitive process in most people we can detach from it and instead discover ourselves by observing our responses to all the manoeuvres.

If we feel sympathy or antipathy, love or hatred, dominance or subservience, approval or disapproval, obliged or guilty, fearful or overexcited, deferential or respected, superior or inferior, as a result of being with another person or in response to an object of attention, there is an imbalance in the flow between us that will affect us in some way. We can ask ourselves if this is the response we wish to give or whether we are being intuitively organized.

Some games are very subtle and silent whereas other games are powerful and noisy. Someone feeling subtly abused may have an argument to bring something to consciousness in the other person or to restore the balance. An onlooker could assume the aggressor to be the manipulator but some apparent victims are actually in control, having learnt their own methods of manipulation or coping with imbalances.

If people have been intuitively playing games to their own benefit they could have enormous resistance to looking at them. Not only do they need to undertake an intellectual exercise with honesty but they may also need to alter their self image or make changes in their thoughts and behaviour without any of it being directly to their benefit.

All healthy children will seek attention to be able to unfold their karmas and achieve their desires through organizing their world. Any manipulation they become involved in can be seen as an indication that they are not getting as much attention as they would like.

Adults may have their main desires fulfilled and are often prepared to swap personal power for some wisdom. As we understand the world better we are able to act from wisdom and consideration of each event and our level of training needn't be as high, or habitual responses needn't take precedence, so that we can sacrifice or redirect much of the energy that was previously tied up in our conditioning.

It is possible, through mutual consideration, for most people's needs to be met without power struggles being necessary. As soon as people accept that success in meeting their needs will be normal, further empowerment of themselves to enable them to be competitive or dominate others will be unnecessary. They and the people around them will be able to relax.

A society where everything in the physical world flows easily so that everyone's needs are easily met, enables people who realize they can easily have enough, to cease empowering their desires or protect themselves from want. They can bring their attention to new levels.

31 Leaders directing the flow.

It is possible for a leader to accept the influence and power of all her people and transcend it, enabling the fulfilment of everyone's needs in the process. She can be more of a distributor/creator than an accumulator/director. Her personal power may be low but because of her relationships to people her access to power in times of need may be considerable.

Followers focus their attention on their leader. This flow of support may be organized through her appearances and lectures or by everyone being given pictures of her to keep in their homes. A leader is then able to direct the flow of life-energy on her communities behalf or to recommend other areas of life that the people can focus on.

Many groups are organized in hierarchies so that each leader who is supported in turn supports others. As a result the people at the top can set the agenda and organize the flow of support from large numbers of people to any activity they wish to focus on, anywhere in the world. Naturally this agenda frequently includes the expansion of their own influence and the recruitment of additional members.

When a leader arises out of the needs of a group it is frequently the case that she is their servant as much as their leader. The roles she plays for her community can be regarded as equal to other roles, so that she does not need to be served but can be co-operated with.

Some leaders who are about enabling the awakening and enlivening of their followers may support a range of life and spiritual options so that tolerance of alternative groups is normal. Leaders who are concerned about their personal power, influence or wealth are inclined to actively encourage antipathy towards their opponents so that no life-energy support is wasted and may flow to them instead.

The process of leadership is a natural one that can have great benefits. Some people work hard at projecting an image that says with this woman everything will be wonderful so that people will seek to serve or assist them. If the leaders do not accept their responsibilities to their group then it is up to the members to ensure a balanced relationship is maintained.

Where we see people as equals it is possible to share our wisdom and love if we choose so that everyone is looked after. When we have strong personal foundations to refer to and only carefully chosen desires we do not need much power.

When the relationship is in balance, the leaders will intuitively look after the interests of the group, and direct the flow according to the groups needs as well. This may require all the members to learn to assert their agendas as well so that gradually everyone can accept responsibility for the leadership role.

32 *Letting go of fear and creating abundance.*

Trust enables people to expand in their energies beyond their own needs, to involve themselves in creative exploration and allows them to share their surplus with others they are connected to. In trust, and with confidence, we no longer need to train ourselves further, and we may let go much of our old training and conditioning and convert the energy, making it available once more. as we are confident in our abilities. In trust we know that we will always have enough so we no longer need to compete or empower our desires or goals.

Fear often causes people to pull in their energy to create better or more powerful training and barriers with which to protect themselves and to reduce their interaction with the world. Fear is always out of balance, either leading to loss of confidence, and the handing over to people who appear confident, or to attempts at controlling the world to prevent being overwhelmed. Areas of openness may be closed down, locking up energy and cutting us off from some of the interflow of life.

When we feel fear we are feeling that we are in danger of losing control or of being abused. Some people feel fear as soon as there is a possibility that they won't be completely dominant or successful. They may have a permanent feeling of not having enough like people hoarding unnecessarily for years after the shortages of a war.

Fear forces us to give attention and life-energy to these vulnerable areas to further reinforce them or to give them a new patterning. If we constantly struggle to protect ourselves from fear, or if we engage in long term training, we can accumulate our life-energy resources so that when we reach a position of trust in ourselves or completion we can feel we have an abundance. How far we train ourselves with thought, practise or empowering desires is a personal affair but in doing so it is worth acknowledging that we are detracting from other areas of ourselves or our community.

Talented people often naturally accumulate an abundance as their training can be through interest and enjoyment rather than insecurity so they can remain more balanced, leading to more confidence. If we feel ourselves training due to fear it is worthwhile dealing with the fear rather than the protection or training.

Some people have periods of confidence and plenty where they may see themselves as an earth mother type, being able to continually give out of their own abundance until they have depleted their resources. They may then burn out or harden their hearts to close off from others to save themselves, perhaps withdrawing too far for a while. People who had been unconsciously benefiting may have come to expect it so that their attempts at coming to balance may be perceived as letting them down.

After a major conversion experience, or kundalini, the energy available may make it possible for all desires to be instantly, and magically, satisfied, organizing physical events intuitively, to do so. The individual may feel like a "god" until they have depleted their power, and come back to earth.

When people have lived for a long time with high levels of trust they may have few parameters in place or little training in any physical or social skills so that they can be easily influenced by anyone with a strong ego or purpose. Competition, and the training it brings, has a benefit of ensuring that minimum protection is available to everyone through their own vigilance, or trained responses.

When there are ego battles, feelings of fear will be frequent as the power needed to stay dominant escalates. Individual protection is far more difficult than mutual protection in a harmonious group. Competition is successful in achieving goals because, through fear of failure, all parties dedicate all their energy to a single area of life, but it keeps their lives narrowly focused.

In times of vulnerability, due to exhaustion or illness, our resources may be depleted and we can be open to suggestions, spiritual trespass and to the fear that can result. When we have a surplus of life-energy we may not be concerned about losing a little and will have an additional meal if necessary or take time off to relax. In times of stress we are at the edge of our limit so that small losses can disturb and disorientate us easily.

In confidence we can go out knowing we can deal with anything we encounter. True confidence based on self knowledge enables individuals to relax as they know that life has its minor fluctuations. False confidence and fear, however, often alternate as people discover at times that they don't have enough for their times of uncertainty, discover fear anew and seek to protect themselves again.

Many people respond to fear with their will power, pushing themselves through. As a result they may be continuing to empower their fears or aversions, as well as their will to overcome, tying up their resources. Instead they can explore the fear and let it go, so that no will power is needed to act and they are free to do as they wish.

As we relax and trust we can choose to hand over more responsibility to our conditioned body allowing much of our lives to continue automatically. At the same time the surplus this allows us enables us to observe all that we are involved in, including our intuitive responses, so that we can act in the moment whenever we wish. By relating in this relaxed way with awareness we are able to maintain a surplus of goodwill to share as necessary.

By enabling someone else to relax, to trust themselves and let go of other issues and unconscious conflicts, we enable them to enthusiastically concentrate on their area of interest and be more effective in what they do.

Confidence, usually based on self knowledge, appropriate training and a surplus of life-energy, enables us to be the master of areas of life we dedicate ourselves to, so that other people will be intuitively influenced or protected by us in those areas. This influence is based on our level of confidence whether we have mastered completely those areas of life or not.

A juggler can master, and bring into subconscious control, a range of tasks he can perform concurrently. The level of concentration needed to learn the basic skill may be beyond some people. However if they open up to learning it intuitively from the master it may be much easier. Anyone who refines themselves in any area of life refines their whole community in that area to some extent as well. In confidence people with knowledge, dreams or skills can share intuitively. In trust we can open up to it and learn easily.

Some people are perfectionists not being content to let go of conscious control until they are the best. The perfectionist directs a lot of energy now so that if he needs to use the skill or knowledge it will be powerfully available later. He may be a specialist in a narrow area and become the resource person for his community, intuitively guiding everyone in his area. His role can be based on knowing something thoroughly but this requires a preparedness for self sacrificing many of life's other possibilities.

Systems people explore until they are confident they know the basic principles and then move on to something else. A systems person can have a basic familiarity of most of human knowledge or abilities. When needed he can, by providing the energy, work out or recall whatever he needs or intuitively receive it from his community if his foundation knowledge or abilities are in place. His confidence is based on the knowledge that he has access to anything he needs.

33 *Choosing to share the flow.*

When we observe other peoples games and imbalances, and our own, we can come to see them for what they are and play them out, or if we choose we can adjust them or be detached from their effects. As we become more balanced ourselves we can do this with people who may be closer to us and participate in a relaxed way. By letting go of unwanted habitual responses, we can act in the moment.

Detachment is not a lack of emotion, it is a coming to truthful emotion where we respond truly to situations rather than allow other people to take advantage of their knowledge of our conditioning, vanities or desires, and evoke emotional responses in us according to their own desires or needs.

We can choose to experience emotion, and to be fully engaged in it, or we can acknowledge something for what it is and choose our own response, or experience humour or sadness. Instead of responding in the expected way, we can ask ourselves what we would like to evoke in them to change the atmosphere or relationship, and to find a suitable means to do this.

Detachment is not an easy attitude to develop. It is more likely to be a consequence of personal clarity, self knowledge, self confidence and security where we no longer have any need to be involved.

Once we are detached, not habitually connected, a flow no longer needs to occur between us and other. We could enthusiastically share an interest, support them in compassion or affection or if we wish we could choose to keep our energy to ourselves.

Often people are allowing unfinished business from their past or their groupsoul to flow through them so that it may not be relevant to us at that moment at all. By being detached we can allow these forces to be expressed or come to consciousness rather than fixing them or forcing them to be repressed.

Detachment becomes more possible when we start to focus on the spiritual aspects of a person or event, rather than on the appearances. This will help us see things for what they are rather than what other people want us to see. In knowing that we are all playing out the forces flowing through us we can remember the whole of the person, or ourselves, rather than be caught by their expressions of the moment.

When a leaf is ready to die it falls from the tree. when we no longer need our relationship with someone we can become detached from them. As long as we are out of balance we can resonate with other people who share that imbalance, whether it is a desire or an aversion, an interest or a fear. When detached we can continue our relationship out of affection or appreciation rather than need.

Our complementary needs can come to completion from our mutual interplays. Together we have allowed each other to explore that area of life and to master it or to let it go.

If we attempt to disconnect rather than let go, we may remain out of balance and lose the opportunity. Instead of the relationship running its course it may go underground and become more intense in the minds of the individuals until they pull each other in, to interact again. To complete the imbalance some method will need to be found, either with the person or with someone else.

While we can learn by going through our imbalances there are also times when we can withdraw from a relationship or event if we feel that rather than coming to balance through it, we are being overwhelmed or will be further disturbed by it.

Sometimes it is worth attempting to disconnect from someone, as it is at this time that we feel the forces flowing from them as a separate force. Before this the forces may all be so familiar that they feel to be our own. We can choose detachment or we can choose involvement and allow ourselves to become emotionally engaged again but in new areas in a new way.

When we have eliminated many of the sources of conflict in our lives so that we can be detached from most people and events, there is little intuitive flow between us and the world so that what remains can have a disproportionate influence on us. This is a position commonly recommended by spiritual leaders who encourage their followers to become detached from other areas of their life so that they will not be distracted from their spiritual path.

By being connected to a range of people, we have an abundance of options available to choose from. We may share many of their imbalances but we will also be involved in and enjoy the play of life in the process.

In the interactions with different parts of our community we are exploring different aspects of ourselves. Retiring from the world is beneficial in digesting what we have learned but it means that our supply of new possible physical experiences comes to an end so that for the benefits to be continuous we need to have already developed ourselves far enough in our minds to be able to continue experiencing the world with our spirits.

When we are detached we may lose all purpose for having relationships. There may be no flow between us and nothing learned. It is through our interactions that we usually restore balance. Once off balance we could remain that way until someone stepped in.

Whole communities can be out of balance for generations if no one is able to transcend the inappropriate forces, and the patterns of behaving or thinking, become permanent. An individual can remove his own imbalances if separate from his community but for it to benefit his community he may need to merge with it once more or at least to dip in to it when able.

The ability to see people or events as they are, enables us to detach from them and to choose our involvement. Detachment can be a tool to reorganize our lives, rather than a means to escape from life.

CHAPTER SIX

BEING CHALLENGED

BY THE

INTUITIVE FORCES

Intuitive action, with common sense, can lead to harmony with the needs of our group, whereas acting in freedom as an individual enables us to create our lives as we choose. There is, and there always will be, this dynamic between ourselves and our groups, so that there will be times when we can accept, the suggestions and impulses we receive spiritually, and others when we will need to assert ourselves.

34 Being organized by the flow.

We are all spiritually organized by our spouses, parents, friends, employers, and people in power or authority. It is part of the process of intuitive cooperation in a community and of parental direction and protection of children.

If we are creating possibilities with our minds that other people are intuitively receiving and responding to, then what they send back to us may arrive intuitively as well. To be able to have what we ask for in our thoughts, desires, prayers and visualizations, we may need to intuitively co-operate with people trying to assist us.

Impulses and feelings can organize actions and thoughts for us, long after we have forgotten their purposes. If we feel ourselves being directed we can increase our vigilance and observation but still co-operate, if we have the time and energy. To ignore all impulses that have no rational explanation can alienate us from intuitive cooperation and prevent the serendipitous fulfilment of our goals.

Our intuition can provide us with an ever increasing number of possibilities while our conscious discernment can reduce them as our conscious resources are only a fraction of what we can have access to. We can bring the accumulated wisdom of our whole group or of generations of people to our every action if we allow our intuition to operate.

Intuitive action, with common sense, can lead to harmony with the needs of our group whereas acting in freedom as an individual enables us to create our lives as we choose. There is and there always will be this dynamic between ourselves and our groups so that there will be times when we can accept and others when we will need to assert ourselves.

When we feel well supported by our community we can assume that our impulses, inspirations and intuition will be valuable. In times of change or uncertainty we may connect up to people who's spiritual involvement in our lives may not be appropriate so that our level of discernment and vigilance may need to increase for a while.

When we have thoughts, desires, impulses or feelings, we need not be concerned whether they are ours or not but we can ask whether they are valuable to us now or not.

Problems that can be referred to as possession arise when the influences we receive are inappropriate for us or are actively against those we would choose for ourselves and we are unable to discern them in time or to assert ourselves against them. These foreign influences could be impulses to act in new ways or be more subtle and alter our beliefs and goals so that our spontaneous choices are changed.

35 Illness and crime as expressions of imbalance in the flow

Communities are dynamic with every person in them interconnected so that there is a constant spiritual flow of suggestions and support between them all that intuitively alters each members self image, attitude and range of options and limitations.

Just as individuals can be out of balance in their own bodies with areas of congestion and depletion, whole communities can be. On a social level imbalances may appear as pockets of negativity, apathy, aggression, arrogance, impoverishment, guilt, selfishness or their opposites. I have mentioned the negative qualities here but their opposites are also out of balance. While positive qualities are usually of value to the group they can be at too great a cost to the individual.

Any of the whole range of inappropriate attitudes that an individual can feel, can become a common and permanent ingredient of a group.

The process of sharing the flow is a mutually beneficial one, enabling a whole community to continue harmoniously. As a result of the intuitive flow all of us contain our groups and potentially each one of us contains, or has access to, the whole of humanity. We can accept positive or negative ingredients according to what we focus on and contribute to the flow as we choose.

There are people who create more forces with their beings than they ever express. They may empower and repress many of them, making them psychically available to people with a personal shortage of ideas, images or impulses, who may rely on what is available intuitively. How valuable the spiritual contribution of these people is, depends on the quality of the impulses and attitudes they create, and the relevance of them to the people receiving them.

People who are accepted as leaders have greater access to influencing their groups, as people are far more open to them. Problems arise when the powerful individuals with the surplus of possibilities, have negative attitudes which they don't express or balance so that inappropriate forces become active in the group's collective mind. All kinds of desires, prejudices, longings, aversions and obsessions attempt to find their way to expression through other people.

The creator of the forces may not express what he creates because, while he may allow them as thoughts or desires, he may see the actual expression of them as inappropriate and use self discipline to stop himself. Instead the forces may flow through to weaker or less discerning individuals in the community who may suffer or express them on his behalf. This misalignment between empowered desires, and physical expression of them, can be remedied when we accept the reality of our spiritual activities and learn to accept responsibility for our own thoughts or desires or find a way to express our imbalances.

If we are naturally dominant, then people will often take notice of our thoughts or attempt to spiritually obey our requests as our thoughts and desires may be broadcast with the authority of wisdom or the force of orders. Most people wish to please the people they respect and this attempt at goodwill can be accidentally abused.

Each time we feel or have thoughts of criticism or disapproval or inappropriate suggestions, demands or advice, about or for a person, we know that we might be diminishing them, if they are vulnerable to our influence. With positive supporting thoughts and images of other people we enable their successes as we give them confidence in themselves. If our own agendas are in harmony with our groupsoul's then any participation by others will also be to their own benefit.

People who constantly call out spiritually for assistance can also disturb a whole community as many people intuitively respond to cries for help as parents would, and their lives are interrupted as a result. The call for assistance could be for any perceived need, from support for business success, even after making millions of dollars, to fears of danger, ill health or misfortune.

Individuals who receive unbalanced forces intuitively, may express them through their behaviour in co-operation or subservience if they are positive or as crimes if they are not. Their attempts at assisting could also be undermining them through the conflicts that are created within themselves or the loss of life-energy that can result.

While some crimes are premeditated and in harmony with the individuals being, many are intuitive expressions, of other people's forces, in times of weakness or inattention.

If the whole of a community is in harmony then few of its individuals will be far out of balance and illness or crime will be uncommon. The type of illness and crime expressed by members of a community can indicate the kind of imbalance that the community is struggling with.

Different people learn in different ways so that some remain almost unaffected by what they receive through their souls or minds whereas others are so sensitive to it that a simple image received can create major changes in their lives or the most outlandish impulse can be acted out without thought or recognition.

Some people act intuitively and perhaps inappropriately without really intending to. In a protected community these people may always have been guided suitably because there were few, if any, inappropriate impulses available. In the presence of many negative influences available to them today, their behaviour can become more inappropriate. Even when they are consciously aware of the law the intuitive forces flowing through them may be dominant.

Many mental illnesses such as schizophrenia, neurosis, psychosis, compulsiveness or obsessions, are frequently the result of an inability to give an appropriate response to the thoughts, feelings and impulses that are received or arise. There can be a range of imbalanced responses from complete openness to suggestions, reempowerment of inappropriate impulses due to fear, to an attempt to control every detail of their life, to avoid being affected by what is received from the flow.

It is often difficult to identify the sources of an imbalance. The inappropriate forces or patterns could have been accepted long in the past but only be arising in times of vulnerability, or may have been received in the moment of expression. In many ways the source is irrelevant as the solutions can be the same.

A common response to illness or crime is to treat the individual expressing them but it is also valuable to heal the community that it is occurring in.

When a person is too open to the flow, they can be assisted to reduce their vulnerability by reducing stress, bringing order and health back to their lives and inspiring them to nurture their souls. They can also learn to deal with what they receive from the flow by strengthening and balancing their egos. This can be assisted by improving their discernment through relevance, or reality, testing so that they consciously explore anything new that they receive and make a new choice before accepting or acting it out.

To heal a community we need to work with those people who are currently healthy to enable them to come to balance and deal with imbalances on other people's behalf, healing their families and communities in the process. Strong individuals who can allow into themselves some of their communities inappropriate forces can transform or transcend them. In healing themselves in body and mind, they make available to their communities, new healthy responses and their positive patterns.

Some communities attempt to stay healthy with their practices of meditation and prayer, through which individuals actively create a surplus of life-energy to share with others and ensure that their own forces are kept positive and appropriate.

A healthy spiritual or mental atmosphere in a community will make unnecessary the expression of imbalances by the vulnerable members as they will be better supported and receive positive impulses instead.

36 *Intuitive forces expressed through children*.

We may have desires for answers, people or objects, that we send out into our groupsoul or groupmind. Eventually something comes back in response to our requests but we may not be receptive to it so that these forces may find an alternative way to us. Often the easiest way is through children, who's barriers to the transpersonal are more open.

Without knowing why, children often make statements, ask questions, pick up books or objects, go through actions, or make up stories that enable something, that we have started, to be completed. When it finally gets to us we may not recognize what the child is presenting to us or needing to tell us, in response to our thoughts and questions.

While most of what children express intuitively is valuable they can also be open to negative forces. Children, or most people after traumas, have few barriers to irrelevant or inappropriate material flowing to them and it will take time to learn discernment.

A parents ego, connected to the child to diminishing extents until they become independent, can protect the child from much of the unwanted material. If a parents or friend's thoughts are fully confident, positive and supportive there is less chance of negativities coming to the child and they enable the child to naturally unfold their own positive forces.

If a child has an accident, or acts badly in trespass of others, we might ask what it was that allowed or made the behaviour occur. While the adult present may not be the cause, they may have participated or allowed it to some extent. Frequently the forces at work in events are too powerful and diverse for any individual to control alone, and this is particularly so with children.

As adults we may wish to deal with a child's vulnerability by teaching them discernment or giving many rules but they may be too young for this. Sometimes by forcing a child to attempt analytical or intellectual processes we make them more vulnerable.

We can assist vulnerable children by providing an orderly and familiar environment in which they can be comfortable. All routines, habits, consistent rules, and repetitive tasks also train the child's etheric body so that they are strengthened and their vulnerability to chaotic or inappropriate impulses is reduced.

By allowing them to participate in their family's activities from an early age children are drawn more powerfully into their groupsoul. As a result they are more easily protected intuitively by their families as well.

By ensuring the images that actively work in the child, from books or television, are positive and nurturing, we can help children to develop positive discernment intuitively.

The orderly homelife of the past ensured that children were well protected, but they may have been over trained instead. This often deprived them of an ability to be flexible. Many modern children are too thin-skinned which may help to keep up with change but can also deprive them of a chance to build their personal foundations successfully. It is possible to give children the best of both routines and diversity, by ensuring a place for both in their lives.

37 Community influences and the individual.

In times of war, depression or drought people may become so intensely aware of doing without that they very powerfully create desire forces to make sure they never go without again and may become hoarders of food for the rest of their lives.

A sense of urgency resulting from real or imaginary trauma, or the threat of it, can enable a whole nation to blindly follow particular directions, which are promised as the saviour of the day. These forces are taken in deeply and continue long after they are valuable or necessary.

Leaders often create false beliefs to stimulate their people to actively follow particular courses of action. Such things as security, efficiency, employment, accountability, material wealth, saving, spending, health care, education or training, freedom of speech, going to church, smoking, drinking, playing sport, while all able to be valuable, are often focused on to the detriment of other areas of life or human potential. As a result individuals frequently accept priorities which are personally unreal or out of proportion.

These examples are obvious but we are all out of balance in hundreds of more subtle areas due to belonging to a community in which particular beliefs, fears, desires or aversions are held as real or essential. For most people, how they fill their minds and time is culturally determined rather than personally chosen.

The intuitive flow through a community can gradually align all the agendas and beliefs as a means of bringing about harmony, independently of the value of the beliefs. These patterns can guide all of the individual's attention and thinking and they may have difficulty even recognizing anything that doesn't fit.

Due to the plurality of forces there is a constant breathing occurring throughout the community, expansions of some forces and contractions of others. We are directed, through many streams of influence to focus on different areas of life at different times as the organism of humanity gradually unfolds, blossoms or awakens.

Through the artificial creation of fears, aversions or unreal desires the natural process of adjustment can be blocked so that imbalances continue or become more extreme. Before social change is possible inappropriate, intuitive, social parameters may need to be recognized and set aside, so that something new can enter.

A fear of hell and a desire for heaven, while once being valuable as social controls, now block the natural human development and the exploration of individual free will. We have all accepted many parameters intuitively that limit us, and people that we are connected to, needlessly.

Social harmony can result from the blind obedience to patterns or laws, or each individual can be awakened to the possibilities and benefits of conscious co-operation with consideration of consequences for themselves and others. Every individual, by becoming aware of the flow of life and their possible role in it, can make conscious choices about their personal thoughts, desires and actions and in the process have a creative effect on the unfolding of their community.

Allowing ourselves to be carried along by the flow may lead to harmony but if there is no wisdom the changes or agendas may only be expressions of imbalance and it will be necessary for someone to rise up to question the social directions. If we all attempt to do this in our own areas then collectively we may be able to create a new world.

Our abilities in spiritual realms are active now. Individually we can bring ourselves to balance and awaken to the new levels of human possibility. Our belief systems not only organize our lives for us, they also restrict the natural unfolding of our human potential. Everything imaginable is possible so we can all choose the best.

38 Being directed by our groupsoul.

We may have been part of our groupsoul since before birth so that the types of desires we have and the limitations we impose on ourselves and others may have been accepted without thought from our group. In the sense that we are still allowing ourselves to be directed by our conditioned or desire bodies without having made these completely our own we could say that we are possessed by our groupsoul. It is possible to come to act from our selves so that we assertively balance our own needs and aspirations with the needs of our groupsoul's.

We can at any time join new groups so that our groupsouls can change as well. To varying extents we are inducted into every group we join, whether it is a social, work, sporting, religious or political group. To be part of a group usually requires that in many areas we are intuitively in agreement with it. Unless this is so people will be out of harmony with each other and the conflict can be disempowering for everyone.

We may choose our group very carefully but on joining or continuing to belong to a group we allow ourselves to be possessed by some of the group's qualities rather than choosing all of our own. On leaving we may also intuitively, or even with great relief, jettison much that we had previously accepted.

Gradually we all take in more deeply whatever we are involved in so that if we leave after many years we may be unable to differentiate between who we are ourselves and what we became through the role or group we were in.

When we spend time with a different group that is not accepted by our own we naturally come to appreciate many aspects of the people and to gradually expand ourselves into valuing their " odd " agendas, attitudes and beliefs. However when we cease to focus on them and are back in our old group it is possible, if we are not strong enough, to return to the old prejudiced positions. This flexibility is particularly the case for teenagers and other people experiencing transitions and life changes who have not learnt to act from personal foundations yet.

By simply remembering either group we can tune ourselves into their position and be able to compare them and choose for ourselves, gradually finding ways to transcend conflicting positions. Rather than living a schizophrenic existence between the two groups it becomes possible to integrate the different influences according to our own expanded world view.

Individuals acting as bridges between groups enable the development of tolerance and even acceptance of one group by an other. Through individuals struggling to reconcile differences it is possible for them to get to know themselves, separate from the influence of either group.

39 Being dominated by our groupmind.

A groupmind consists of people who share a common interest, profession, trade or craft. As we focus our attention on any area of life we connect up to aspects of other people who are also interested in it. Anyone who has trained and saturated themselves in particular subjects or skills, whether practical, conceptual or imaginary, has developed a habitual connection and become permanent members of that groupmind. Once we are trained in anything we can respond intuitively to anyone who focuses on our area of interest, without needing it to come to consciousness to explore and share it.

Groupminds have people who have been trained without thought and others who have true understanding. If a groupmind is shared by exploring, creative people it will continually be developing as people contribute to it from new experiences or other areas of life. If all of its contents have been organized or completed it will no longer be open to change so that people can become stuck in particular forms of seeing their roles, purposes and methods. The process of organization of any field of endeavor almost inevitably leads to standardization and then stagnation. Fortunately this creates a pressure of its own leading to a new impulse.

Whole communities, societies and even civilisations can become possessed by their groupminds once the contents have been taken deeply into their groupsoul. At this level the contents are all habitual and intuitive rather than fluid and open to conscious change. It is often easier to develop new groupminds than to alter a long established one. To avoid getting caught in the old mold we will need to approach the same area of life from a new perspective or direction, to freshly explore it.

Any new discovery in life begins in excitement and creates change. Once it has been assimilated it becomes part of the social patterning where it is seen as unchangeable. A new spiritual impulse is at first liberating but through the gradual assimilation, it forms a new intuitive framework. Religions, fields of knowledge of science, medicine, education, economics, technology all have periods where they enable liberation but eventually they hold their communities back so that completely new systems need to be invented regularly to enable community life to continue to flow.

Through the course of human awakening there have been a variety of cosmo-conceptions, methods of organizing societies and ways of fulfilling the needs of the people. In their essences each groupmind still remains in existence and can be evoked and entered so that their patterns and forces can live in the people involved in them. There also groupminds which are in their infancy that are being explored but which are beyond the abilities of most people to deal with yet.

In being obsessive in any area of life we are continually opening ourselves further to that subject, so that the flow with it continues to grow. While this can be very valuable in learning and exploring it can be destructive if we are no longer able to close off from it. Instead of moving our attention freely through a range of different life experiences we can become stuck exclusively on particular ones.

Each of us can move our attention through different groupminds and what we become involved in will differ according to where and how we focus. We can saturate ourselves with areas of life and live in the past, present or future groupminds. There is value in having a range of possibilities to compare, as this can lead to personal freedom, but on a personal level we can have our lives brought out of harmony with our own communities as a result. Dominance by our groupminds is a form of possession whether it enables our lives and community harmony or not.

If people focus on anything with aversions or fear they will be connected to negative aspects of groupminds so that these can come to live strongly in them and become fascinating. Negative groupminds can come to absorb people's minds as powerfully as positive ones and the lives of whole communities can come to be dominated by them. These states can arise most easily in times of fear, chaos or poverty.

In confidence we can choose from the best of life. What we create or allow with our minds comes to interact with every event we are involved in, affecting everyone we are connected to as well. We can choose to be inspired and inspiring by directing our attention positively.

40 Possession by an individual.

Most adult's egos are able to go beyond their own needs at times and contribute to their communities or individuals they focus on. They may assist with spiritual healing, teaching, guiding or co-operatively creating future events.

If we are strongly connected to powerful people we could be well supported but we could also be intuitively dominated by them so that we act against our own interests or suffer the conflict of struggling against them.

When a person is supported by his community, even if possessed, the forces flowing through him will be suitable to his community, and it may never be apparent that his ego is weak and that he is not the master of his life. However if he comes under the influence of other people astrally, at times when he is without sufficient protection from his group, his behaviour could become as bizarre as the people directing him astrally, wish to make it.

When we speak to any person they have their whole groupsoul or their mentor with them spiritually if necessary while they respond. They may act totally on behalf of their group. If the group support and influence is appropriate then the person can be very strong in the world but if it is inappropriate then he may come into conflict that alone he is unable to get out of because he doesn't have the personal foundations to refer to in consciousness.

Any person who is overly focused on us with their own agendas can be seen as possessing us if their influence is contrary to our own intentions. This may not be evident to any physical observer but many people are open in their choices to their own cost.

When we are open to particular individuals there will be a flow between us. This can be intuitively regulated and be to our benefit. Sometimes, however, one of the people focuses persistently on the other with directions rather than options, either directing their lives or creating spiritual warfare with them. If there is continuing spiritual dominance it is possible for the weaker person to lose themselves and come to follow obediently. This may have been of value in the context of a monastic community or army but it is always destructive to a person's individuality.

The range of individuals who possess others excessively, can include anyone but typically mothers, teachers, hopeful lovers, scorned lovers, leaders with powerful agendas or people with strong desires that need others to satisfy them. People who are seeking a role that they are yet to have enough clients for, such as healers, counsellors, professional advisers, and private teachers, can all have an imbalanced interest in the lives of the people they are connected to. Typically sales people and politicians are always seeking to have a greater share of influence over other people.

The possession is invariably caused by a combination of one person being overly vulnerable and another having a strong desire to help, serve, learn, sell, lead, advise or to have a pupil or assistant. Where two individuals have complementary needs or regularly focus on each other in an active directed way, the influence can be mutually valuable. Both people will need to remember that if they are intensely focused on the other too often, their connection can easily get out of balance, so that one person will spiritually come to dominate or possess the other.

Possession by individuals is usually a two way affair so that both people can be supported or diminished through it. Stopping the possession can happen at either end, by one of the individuals bringing themselves to balance or disconnecting from the other person. If people are stuck in their focus on someone else it is usually because of an imbalance in their attitude to them, such as fear or desire. By broadening their options and enabling a real view of the person or situation the imbalance can be overcome and their focus of attention freed.

If someone is focused on us excessively we can give them telepathic suggestions to read a book or occupy themselves in some way, enabling them to shift their attention or come to balance about us. A common cause of fixations of attention is fear and confusion where the person is overwhelmed to the point of being unable to assert their ego and move their attention themselves.

Many people are able to spiritually guide others either consciously or intuitively and if they do so with true consideration of the persons needs it can be temporarily very valuable as a means to an end.

41 *Collective patterning and the reoccurrence of events.*

Plants follow patterns precisely with few new individual desires or opportunities of their own for choosing or changing. Animals have their patterns but also have a capacity for diversity in their responses and their own desires. People have patterns, a capacity for diversity and an ability to desire and create their own futures and to consciously choose a new response to every event which arises.

Our etheric body through its patterns organizes all of our bodily functions and intuitive responses and behaviour. All of our habits, routines, beliefs and all of our conditioned responses operate at this level. We continue to follow formed patterns until we change them, through willed physical activities, with our desires finding new possibilities, or in consciousness deciding again.

Much of human social life is also organized in this way, through the development of roles, agendas, life purposes, religions and forms of government and community services all being organized into patterns of responses so that they continue without further need for consideration.

How we perceive the world, and what aspects of it we focus on, also follows patterns. Just as our physical bodies continue with great complexity and subtlety without needing conscious input at any time most aspects of community life do too.

With training we can bring our awareness to every cell and activity of our bodies and make conscious changes to them or to the systems that govern them. We can also do this with every aspect of our society and our relationship to the cosmos so that theoretically we could free ourselves of many of the intuitive patterns if we wished or needed to.

Patterns are expressed in our every word, gesture and movement, in all of our choices and are blended in with our desires forces with which we create our future events. In some ways every feature of our physical body and every, thought desire and action we express is an indication of the patterns we hold and impose on the world so that by observing these we can at times predict analogous patterns in other areas of our lives.

While we can pursue new desires or live in the moment much of the time we all follow our patterns automatically so that our every attitude and response can be directed by them.

Our patterns are all interconnected with the patterns of other people so that many of our interactions and much of our lives can be organized by them so that even our conversations and relationships usually follow predictable sequences, if we allow them to. We all intuitively play our parts to ensure that harmony is maintained.

The intuitive patterns of responses we all hold can be to particular events but they can also be evoked by different times of the day, week, month, year or at different stages and ages of our life.

Some of these patterns are universal to all humans while others may be personal or belong to our family or groupsoul. At particular times we may feel the need to change our life, fulfill a project or to follow a course of action which is separate from any rational reason.

While we may feel limited by our conditioning it is usually useful and to be conscious in all of the activities of each body is impossible. However at times individuals, families or societies take on patterns which are not useful but which direct and limit them for a while. This is particularly the case with traumas of any kind which create an intensity in the forces of the patterning far beyond normal events.

Imbalances resulting from personal or social traumas become a part of the cultural heritage of a people and often patterns that individuals learnt to enable them to cope with their traumas are passed unconsciously onto their children even when they are no longer relevant.

Traumas that parents underwent at particular stages of their life can be unconsciously passed on to their children so that at similar stages of life they too will have to undergo similar traumas in an attempt to deal with them on behalf of the family.

The patterns lead to creative forces bringing about events as well as organizing the responses of the people involved. Until someone can discover and acknowledge the inappropriate patterning and restore the balance position it will continue generation after generation.

When there has been a trauma which has destabilized an individual or community for a while the problem area is focused on with intensity and the solution is taken in deeply and passed on intuitively to other people in the groupsoul. When it is a valuable solution this process can be wonderful as the whole community can benefit easily. Archetypes or prototypal patterns are created in this way.

Most patterns are taken on intuitively. If we were conscious of taking them on we would often choose not to, as in many cases their value is not apparent until a situation evokes them and they play their part. Every new experience in life which stirs the emotions can be taken into our patterning body to some extent to affect our future events and our responses to them.

Each pattern has a time of creation and a trigger to enable it to arise, as well as a method of being completed or altered. This is most obvious with our habits and beliefs which can at times be exceptionally strong but still come to an end. Sometimes the pattern created is a creator of further imbalances in itself. It may contain the fear of the event and be a force for bringing about future identical events where the individuals will both organize the negative creation as well as deal with it inappropriately, so that a negative pattern can be further entrenched. In themselves the patterns are independent of ethics or obvious benefits and consist of anything that has undergone the process of acceptance.

Many of the patterns we have are inherited through the influence of our groupsoul and may not be recognized at all. By associating with people who are different to us there can be an intuitive conflict of these etheric patterns, so that some of them can come to consciousness to be reassessed.

New ways of life are a result of an abandonment of old patterns and a replacement with new ones. The tenacity of our old patterns is such that to remove them is an arduous process except with traumas, initiations or religious conversions during which they can be rapidly shed or disempowered. In removing patterns we can also affect other related karmic forces so that we are usually more inclined to improve, broaden or redirect our patterns than to dispose of them lightly.

Often the exploration and recovery process is done on a cultural level. By looking at the popular movies, songs and stories it is possible to see what it is that a community is trying to come to terms with or to create new patterns in. The process of collective patterning itself has enabled man to keep the best of all we have learnt as foundations for further human development.

CHAPTER SEVEN

BALANCING OUR

PARTICIPATION

IN THE FLOW.

When we, and our relationships, are in balance we can trust that all will be well in our lives and that unconsciously, out in other realms our spirits are creating a wonderful future and protecting us from unfavourable events. This is a great position to be able to be in and can be a usual one.

By redirecting our attention to new areas of life or higher realms or ideals, we would begin attracting new people to us on a spiritual level. This also weakens our links with those people we are connected to who do not share our common focuses of attention.

42 *Balancing our spiritual connections.*

Children are, by necessity, and to their advantage, out of balance in their relationships with parents. While parents support their children, they are still dominant in most ways with a child learning many games in an attempt to be dominant in others.

Our society is hierarchically organized, mimicking the relationships of parent and child, so that students are usually expected to be deferent to teachers and employees to be subservient to their employers.

If we have habitual responses to people of dominance or subservience, sympathy or antipathy, authority or deference, or any other imbalanced response, our spiritual relationships will be out of balance as a consequence.

As we get older and adopt new roles or responsibilities, we have the opportunity to alter our relationships and intuitive connections with everyone so that the old imbalances can come to an end. With wisdom and harmony a society can be organized with relationships of equality where everyone has a different but valued role.

We can alter our relationship with the world or with the rest of our community. This will in turn affect every person we are connected to. By bringing our selves to balance, or to find and express our own natures, we bring pressure on people in our groupsoul to alter their thoughts, desires, and behaviour as well.

It is a strong person who can make major changes, against the will of his community, and maintain them, while still staying connected. An automatic spiritual power struggle would ensue until new agreements are reached which would reflect the relative power of the people involved in each area. For this reason it is often valuable to ensure that our relationships are in balance, with people we are close to, before making major changes.

If we are feeling overwhelmed by unsuitable influences or drained by what we receive or are required to give, we can bring our relationship to the particular person to balance and reduce the flow.

We can alter what we create with our aspirations and send with our thoughts, desires or needs or alter our responses to them. These changes are usually more valuable in the long term than disconnecting as our relationships are bilateral and attempts to cut off often create more difficulties than they solve. A gradual letting go reduces the flow naturally.

When we, and our relationships, are in balance we can trust that all will be well in our lives and that unconsciously, out in other realms our spirits are creating a wonderful future and protecting us from unfavourable events. This is a great position to be able to be in and can be a usual one.

If we have been having changes and are out of balance, we may temporarily need to take active steps to ensure that we return to balance again. We may need to set aside time to relax or address our own needs each day.

We can have new aspirations long before our habitual responses are changed so that often we are sending a range of mixed signals to people, from our speech, our thoughts, our feelings and desires, our conditioned responses and from our physical behaviour, all at the same time.

Depending on where people operate, they may be affected by us at one level more than others, with everyone being affected differently. By coming to harmony in ourselves we make it easier for others to relate to us as well.

Some people make changes easily from physical interactions but others learn through spiritual experiences so that to change our connections with people we will need to keep this in mind to ensure we are making the changes at the right level, addressing physical behaviour, or observing thoughts, desires and parameters in greater detail.

As people alter their relationship to themselves and their world, they alter their involvement with us as a result. To enable changes in our connections we could inspire them to new possibilities or provide a safe space in which they can let go of their blockages to change. We could also relieve them of their unnecessary burdens, which may be holding them with their attention focused too narrowly, by reassuring or supporting them.

There are many areas of physical or verbal behaviour that could be explored. These include changing what we project through our dress, speech and topics of conversation, changing our attitudes and responses to people, or changing our interests and goals that we try to share with them.

By altering how we physically relate to people we give precise signals to them in consciousness that could be confusing if out of line with our spiritual response. By completing the changes in ourselves first and allowing them to flow through intuitively to both our physical and spiritual activity we will naturally alter our connections with people at the same time.

What is first chosen and empowered in thought can flow through to our imagined responses and creative possibilities and then down into our habitual patterns and physical behaviour.

If we do not alter our historical connections we will continue to receive a flow through or from them which could be in conflict with how we see ourselves now. Some initiations and religious conversions are about destroying much of our conditioning body, and our habitual connections at the same time. This enables us to rebuild our etheric forces in co-operation with our new group and come to harmony with it.

Habitual connections exist on a form level so that we can alter them gradually as we would habits. We can consciously create new patterns of relating and provide the effort and discipline to purposefully let go of the old way.

We have been empowering habits of behaviour or thought for many years and these have been shared with members of our groupsoul. The process of change will be gradual and the changes to our thoughts and desires may not affect our habits or flow through to our actions immediately.

We will need to be vigilant and patient with ourselves and others until we have let go of the old and empowered the new. By continually choosing and visualizing our preferred ways, when we have the time, and then simply observing ourselves in action and choosing anew when we can, knowing that the changes are happening, we allow them to occur naturally.

If our habits are a result of our desires of the past or present we may be better off letting go of the inappropriate desires, interests, fears or aversions instead of using our will power to change.

We can simply acknowledge that our forces that are organizing us are not valuable and disempower them each time they arise. In this way we also begin to operate with awareness of our true feelings and values rather than following irrelevant conditioning.

If we destroy our habitual connections we cut off from the common source of much of our inherent nature. We also lose our chance of intuitively influencing these people as well. We will gradually grow apart, losing the natural support of our original groupsoul.

If we are confident in our personal foundations we will not be influenced by what we receive and instead will influence other people.

If we feel out what we are receiving or have created in the past we can organize our thoughts with consideration of them rather than battling against them. Refining or redirecting our own or our groups soul qualities is more effective than opposing them.

By loosening our habitual connections we also redirect the level of our relationships so that more of it will occur at astral or conscious levels instead where we are in a better position to deal with it.

If we have changed dramatically it is likely that our intuitive foundations will be much weaker than other people's until we have completed making all of our new choices. If many people share common foundations they will mutually support each other and all be powerful as a result. If we do not wish to be intuitively realigned with them we will have to be vigilant until stronger.

If we try to let go of old areas without choosing something new, we may remain connected to the same people and our changes will be constantly modified by their influence.

By redirecting our attention to new areas of life or higher realms or ideals, we would begin attracting new people to us on a spiritual level. This also weakens our links with those people we are connected to who do not share our common focuses of attention.

By having recognizably valuable goals of our own, other people can come to want to adopt or share them, and these can become the new areas we have in common.

We have many habits and desires that lead us into unbalanced connections. These include our desires to help, to obey, to serve, to lead, to create, to love, to know, to have, to be active or to be approved all of which can draw us to inappropriately support or interfere with people spiritually.

Instead we can develop habits of choosing whether we will be involved or not. By doing so we alter our automatic spiritual involvement as well.

By altering how we respond intuitively to people in general we begin to affect our particular personal connections as well, so that where we have always been subservient we may no longer be as easily.

We may first need to first alter our image of ourselves as a helper or to change our beliefs so that we can become detached from people's difficulties and only step in to assist if we choose. If we have difficulties with particular relationships we can redefine them so that we might see a difficult parent as a distant relative instead.

We can also change our level of expectations, obligations, intimacy, availability, the roles we act from, shared interests or focus of attention, so that these are all intuitively realized in our interactions.

Rather than relating from habit or feelings of obligation we can turn our relationships into ones of shared interest where we ignore the historical relationship and focus on what we share of value now. We can focus on our dreams instead of on our memories, leading us into the future together rather than staying in the past.

We can alter our thoughts and desires that relate to our friends or family or anyone we focus on so that intuitively they could feel us out us as friends, assistants, allies or consultants or whatever we are creating in our minds in relation to them.

If we progressively cease thinking about the individual and our mutual interest with them, and cease responding to associations with them, then they will be able to intuitively feel that we are no longer interested in them and they may have less inclination to be with us.

If we wish we can develop new responses in ourselves that people will feel out and intuitively respond to.

By being careful to select only valuable areas to assert ourselves in, whether with our thoughts, desires or actions, we spare ourselves many unnecessary conflicts. If we are confident in ourselves we can open up to anyone but we may no longer need to. Once we are in balance ourselves our connections will usually be in balance too.

43 Coming to harmony after transitions.

Traumas or life changes, whether planned or not, from changing jobs, homes, or partners, having children, retiring or the deaths of people close to us, create a need for a major overhaul in all of our goals and parameters. This may be required by our new demands or those of the group we become a part of. We may do this consciously or accept everything intuitively from our new groups.

If we suffer a trauma or major life change, then all of our attention will be pulled into our inner realms in an attempt to reconcile ourselves to the changes. Our needs, expectations, goals, beliefs and relationships can all be affected and the amount of energy of attention needed for the reconciliation may take our surplus capacity for months as we rebuild our spiritual bodies and our relationships with our community and the world.

During times of trauma or transition our conditioning and desires may be exhausted or set aside. Unless we are able to choose everything in consciousness we may return to a childlike state in our ability to deal with the world.

The trauma can be a debilitating experience leaving us without protection and vulnerable to whatever influence is available. People may attempt to assist or direct us and overwhelm us instead.

While the uncertainty often leads to a level of self exploration that we may not have known before it is precisely at this time that we can discover what we are about. We can see the transition as our chance to create many changes and to redefine ourselves.

Who we are, or are allowed to be, results from a dynamic relationship between ourselves and our groups. We can be brought into alignment with them if we allow it, share a narrow range of the group, or if we are strong enough, or are supported, we can instead have an influence on everyone in the group.

During our times of uncertainty we may lose confidence so that our ability to assert ourselves is diminished. If we have always been confident we may not have been powerfully influenced or even aware of the existence of the group forces before, and may not have learnt how to deal with them.

Almost all experiences require some level of reconciliation with our old positions. If we put these off, by remaining fully focused elsewhere, these can accumulate so that our subconscious demands may increase.

There usually comes a time in mid-life when people have no choice but to reconcile their personal misalignments. Traumas that arise earlier in life create the opportunities for this process to be begun or undertaken earlier.

One of the life purposes of changing groups or roles is this process of creating conflicts between our old positions and the new possibilities. While we may only deal with a part of it in consciousness each time we have a change we have another opportunity to uncover our own soul life, strengthen our egos and discover our h.selves.

Some people can go from one religion, teacher, group or job to another, endlessly with full commitment for a while to each one. A time can come for each of them, however, when they have enough confidence in their own personal foundations to be able to continue, without having to belong to any group or be subservient to any person.

Times of trauma are always demanding of our life-energy and the flow to us is invariably disturbed or redirected involuntarily. People can easily be disoriented by the unexpected changes they feel happening within themselves or in their behaviour.

To reduce confusion through our connections during times of transition, most people intuitively reduce their circle of involvement in life so that they can use what life-energy they receive for their own reconciliation and re-emergence. They may also reduce their connections by limiting their relationships to people they are sure of and who's influence is acceptable to them.

Many people have periods away from their groupsoul so that the intensity of the flow can change and the content can become more positive as they are focused on differently by other people.

Sometimes we need time to choose and establish our personal foundations before returning to the group so that we are stronger in ourselves and can be a source of influence instead or at least participate equally.

44 Supporting someone who is possessed.

Possession occurs whenever an individual expresses or accepts forces that are not their own and that are against their intentions or interest. It is often due to a temporary vulnerability and openness that the individual is unaware of.

Vulnerability can result from a lack of personal development in particular areas that the person meets for the first time, or a removal of protection by a group or parent. It can also be from sickness, exhaustion, demoralization or failure where their ego becomes too weak or their personal discernment is absent.

The individual who is possessed has little choice in the matter as they are dominated by the flow without realizing it. They may regain their freedom when their attention is engaged again but on something else, when the person or group that is possessing them lets go, or when they become strong enough to deal with the forces they are receiving. This could be as soon as their next substantial meal, or after a good sleep.

By linking our egos with people who have disengaged temporarily, are overwhelmed or are confused, we can give them some protection so long as our thoughts are of a neutral or positive nature and suited to them.

Our presence, with people who feel possessed, is sometimes enough to provide them with an ego strength with which they can reorientate and assert themselves.

People who are too full of themselves, their ability to help or their concerns for people, can possess others without realizing it consciously. This kind of possession of a vulnerable individual is common with parents, spouse or members of a prayer group, who are over concerned or out of balance themselves.

Some people may possess others from a distance without realizing. To assist a client we may need to work with the people possessing them. We can do this by sending them positive images of the person they are concerned about to relieve them of worry or to alter the contents of what they are sending out. Sometimes it can help to suggest alternative projects for them to fill their minds with so that they reduce the intensity of the flow to the client.

These changes can be brought about spiritually but in some cases the concerned people will feel discomfort and wish to continue to interfere spiritually or physically, or feel antagonism about the change so that new imbalances may arise.

In the long term it is necessary to help vulnerable individuals to strengthen and balance their egos rather than to deal with the people or forces possessing them.

A denial of the possibility of possession creates problems for people having difficulties. They may be left with no way of relating to inappropriate impulses and they may be further undermined if they believe they are insane. It can be healthier to help them see that their situation has caused them to open up to influences and that they have taken on a few odd thoughts or temporarily acted foolishly.

A few aberrations are easily dealt with but believing themselves crazy can lead to people having a permanently lowered self image which can prevent the assertiveness needed to recover.

Enabling confidence to return is the main method in overcoming any vulnerability to psychic influence. This can be assisted by removing any obvious burdens that are worrying the person, focusing on any positive relaxing area of life or helping them to engage in positive activities.

We can assist people by remembering the best of them rather than responding with fear or negative images of their future. We can remind ourselves that their vulnerability can be temporary, like a cold.

Exorcisms had a place in cultures where people believed that they were powerless before gods and demons and that only through the sacred rituals could they be saved. Exorcisms are not usually relevant today as the rituals are not a part of our normal life. Through the rituals the individual usually handed himself over to be protected by his group, which may not be available or suitable today.

Purification rituals may still be of value as they can help free the individual from fear as this is one of the main causes of remaining vulnerable or focused on a negative area.

Instead of assuming that the forces unbalancing a person are too great, we can see them as still being unexplored or unfamiliar, and assume that eventually the individual will learn to deal with it themselves. If we know the forces we are experiencing as human ones we can feel them as within our ability to deal with.

Some people who hear about etheric, astral or spiritual realms are concerned about possibilities of possession or loss of soul while " away". We are astrally " away" any time we move our attention out to a distant place or time or realm of imagination. We are also etherically present with everything we are connected to so that we can be called to it, if there is an unexpected change there.

In some ways being "away" astrally is like looking at a distant landscape, we might tire ourselves from looking so intently but the only loss of soul would be from a reaction we have to what we see there. In having interests or desires we actively go out into the world astrally and are in fact more alive in our souls from the experience.

Most spiritual experiences are very different from what people expect. As they are often difficult or impossible to reconcile to physical experiences, it is easy to be overwhelmed by them. It is not advisable to attempt to force them unless we are prepared and supported.

If people have spiritual experiences of any kind they can be explained as glimpses into other realms rather than as matters for concern. A positive relationship to the experience can reduce any fear or confusion and allows the person to retain their self confidence. Reverence for our greater human potential leads to openness to positive spiritual experiences whereas fear can lead to negative ones.

If possession occurs it is usually a result of a weakening or temporary absence or withdrawal of our self, ego or soul.

In some respects our soul consists of our desire and conditioning bodies, or their effects. If we have lost our "dreams" or become disillusioned in our life purpose or altered our position in life, so that old beliefs, habits and routines are no longer relevant, we will be vulnerable. These losses can result from overwhelming experiences in any realm including the physical.

The human flame never dies and it can always be rekindled. In fear or self protection it sometimes retreats for a while.

45 *Unfolding our own destinies.*

Through different stages, children organize the development of their physical, etheric, and astral bodies so that their egos and selves can participate more fully in the world.

Until we have come to full self knowledge and self confidence the unfolding of our selves is incomplete so that, to different extents, we are vulnerable to spiritual influences, and imbalances to the flow. Until maturity we can benefit from the spiritual protection of parents, leaders or groups.

While young, we are all exceptionally open. This enables learning and the acceptance of our communities parameters and goals, and an easy intuitive development and harmony with our community. Conscious choice only becomes possible as people approach adulthood and may be delayed until they have developed themselves in other areas first.

If we go straight from acting from our conditioning to consciously acting in consideration of our community, a balance between our own needs and our communities may not be possible. The chaos of our adolescent years is a natural part of developing, strengthening and balancing our ego. Without the chance to be different and explore possibilities, a person's uniqueness may fail to become known to himself or valued. The result could be self sacrifice rather than co-operation.

We could prevent the adolescent expressions, and the development of the ego, with a threat of punishment and force the person to continue to act from their conditioning. If we assist a person to go through their adolescent uprising, whenever in life it may occur, we enable them to come through the egotistical period. By getting to know their selves first they can become adults with the ability to discern, choose, create and initiate.

Until people have explored life and learnt to assert choices, they remain vulnerable to the intuitive influence of their community. Their choices may always be between what they have been conditioned in and what others are suggesting now. As a result the quality of their activities may be totally dependent on their training or the influence of their groupsoul without any personal discernment or contribution.

While acting from our egos we can have personal choice and assert ourselves regardless of the chaos we may cause. After expanding our awareness sufficiently to be able to see our interconnectedness we are able to act from our selves with conscious consideration of our communities. When the mutuality of interests is obvious, and our own needs for security are met, consideration of others is easier.

Once we know ourselves and are confident in who we are we can act with consideration of our own needs and destinies as well as the needs of others.

Rather than compulsively accepting or avoiding duties we can choose duties that suit us, understanding their value and coming to love them for what they enable in our own lives or communities.

Many people do not discover their selves to any great extent in their adolescent years and life's duties often force them to act from conditioning and disregard their own potential. Our current education systems, in many cases, are more about the training of the individual to be an obedient and effective employee than to unfold their personal potential to be human. There are often insufficient opportunities to explore, or have evoked, aspects of our own beings through creative activities in childhood.

The natural awakening of the spirit that could occur in the adolescent years often doesn't, as the person may not have enough access to aspects of their own being or to a range of cultural and social streams to select from. They may also have too few opportunities to assert and find themselves through. As a result this may need to be addressed later in life, to a avoid a trauma or crisis occurring through which an individuals personal forces insist on being heard.

In many ways the more egotistical a person is in their adolescent years and the more of who their "self" is that they know, find or strengthen, the more balanced can be their adult life.

We can benefit from being involved in a variety of groups so that comparisons of possibilities can be made. With each new group we have the option of trading in one lot of conditioning for another or gradually discovering our selves and acting consciously instead.

Depending on where we need to develop ourselves our vulnerability to influence or possession will be different. We may have neglected our physical bodies, so that our spiritual bodies are unable to act through them adequately, or our soul qualities, expressed through our etheric and astral bodies, our ego development or our self discovery.

There is a need for truthfulness and completeness in all that we take into ourselves as any false positions we hold can still organize us and prevent our further awakening.

The scientific view of the world as taught in most primary and secondary schools is very valuable in training people to manipulate the physical world but completely inadequate in preparing them for spiritual experiences.

46 Uncovering our Souls.

Our souls were already with us at birth, with our soul qualities evident in everything we did. These soul qualities can be evoked in response to what we experience through our physical or spiritual senses. They can be expressed through all of our physical or spiritual interactions and preparations, each moment.

Each of us has a diversity of soul aspects that need to breath, taking in through perception and training at times and creatively expressing at others or doing both at once. There can be a flow through every facet of our being.

We can taste the full range of sensory experiences and the emotions, feelings, moods, attitudes, or interests that can be evoked in ourselves and we can nurture new ones.

In living in an unbalanced way it is as if the flow is one way or blocked so that our souls cannot be nourished or participate properly. As a result our emotions may be out of balance or hard to find and the process of exploring new possibilities, or engaging in life, can be difficult.

These personal aspects are our destiny forces that are seeking avenues for expression so that if we habitually deny ourselves we also prevent the completion of our karmic forces.

In some way we are active in astral realms at all times seeking answers and attempting to prepare new events. If we always act from our training or physical needs we deny ourselves a fuller soul involvement.

Working with our soul forces we naturally discover enthusiasm for all we do as our physical activities meet our astral preparations and we can be effective, creative and powerful in the world.

With our imaginations we create possibilities to evoke chosen aspects of our soul life and to feel and express particular emotions and possibilities. If our imaginations have been nurtured and allowed to become full flavored we can have a broad range of aspects with which to participate in spiritual interactions.

Each activity we participate in can be evidence of our soul life with our personal style intertwined with what can otherwise be efficient, practical processes. When we are focused on efficiency our efforts only meet external standards rather than our own need to express something. With imagination we can always lift our involvement to include the needs of the task as well as our own soul or karmic needs for expressing.

Each creation of a product or a service also affects the soul life of each person who receives it. When we know this we can broaden our view of what we are creating and allow ourselves to explore and express our soul qualities and meet this soul need in other people as well.

A building becomes an expression of each person who works on it and a vehicle for evoking a range of soul responses in each person who uses it.

In self sacrifice or subservience we deny ourselves the right to be alive in our souls. When this is continued indefinitely we gradually diminish our other desires, interests and abilities, until it may be hard to find them.

If our possession is through employment it can be as if we have nothing left if we are retrenched from our jobs or retire. We may have completely trained our physical, etheric and desire bodies to the employers or the roles ends. A person can be redirected or demoralized no matter how strong their will if they have poor personal foundations or motivation.

It is possible to work with and teach children with consideration of their personal soul forces. In doing so we enable a natural enthusiasm rather than attempt to block or redirect them with training.

Working with a child's natural forces we empower them. By attempting to impose on them inappropriately we create in them internal conflicts between their own destiny forces and our goals for them, which disempowers them.

By ensuring children are taught from what is true and healthy, on all levels, we provide them with a solid foundation with which to encounter life successfully.

Most of the conditioning we accepted as children is no longer necessary. General principles are often enough in adult life whereas children are often trained very particularly.

We can remove or reshape all unnecessary limitations which include many of our beliefs, rules, desires and goals as these were accepted long before we had any understanding of the world. They can prevent us from finding our own destinies or exploring the world further. By removing the dross of life we allow our own positive soul qualities to arise more easily.

There are many creative activities available today through which we can evoke and explore our own soul life. It often doesn't matter what we choose initially as it is the process of exploration and expression that is important and this can be done in a multitude of ways. In allowing ourselves a diversity of new possibilities we enable a range of possible soul responses to arise in us.

In uncovering our souls we can find much that is valuable but which may create difficulties in our relationships with people. We can find ways to blend in our personal forces with the needs of other people rather than trying to remove or transform them. This can be a challenging process that in laziness or fear we may avoid to our future cost.

Our soul can be expressed in all that we do. We can be powerful in the world but unless we have developed our soul lives this may be of little value to us as it is not meeting our spiritual needs or enabling fulfilment of our beings.

With a strong soul life we do not need much personal power as we are enabled by our personal foundations and flexibility instead. Our spirits work through our soul activities so that if our soul life is rich our spirits can be freer and participate more fully as well.

47 *Strengthening and balancing our Egos.*

With a strong Spirit we can step in and alter our desires or conditioned responses at any time, choose whether and how to be involved in groupminds or groupsouls and live in the moment exploring options and making new choices.

The forces from our past and future and from our community are permanently present. Our egos need to be dynamically interacting with them whenever a change is needed. With choice we can empower, complete with detachment or let go, so that we continually shape the forces we impose on the world in our own way.

Our ego is the fire that tempers all the forces that flow through us and through them enables our own spiritual forces to be expressed. We can continually and gently observe ourselves, participate in the flow as directed or assert ourselves whenever necessary. With a strong healthy ego we can choose whether to assert, self sacrifice, share or withdraw, each moment. In egotism or egolessness we are unable to relate in a balanced way.

To maintain a healthy ego we usually need to have a well organized astral, etheric and physical bodies as well. With a balanced ego we can direct our astral activity in a considerate way so that spiritual co-operation becomes possible. Otherwise our desires can flow through without consideration of consequences to ourselves or others.

Some people are unable to maintain their attention in the physical world, even if awake. They may often be " out of it", "away" or "deep" in thought without realizing. Their ego may not be strong enough to keep their attention in both realms at once or their inner demands may dominate. Low self esteem or distraction are normal with or after trauma, fear, disillusionment, exhaustion and stress. Coming to consciousness in the physical world is a gradual process and some people take longer to incarnate or never do completely.

While many women have well developed soul qualities many of them have not been adequately assisted in developing their egos. Their emotions may be well beyond their abilities to direct or choose, creating difficulties or chaos for them, both in the moment and by being involved in conflicting astral preparations.

Men may not have any difficulty in asserting themselves when necessary, but they may fail to express their own soul forces because these are not sufficiently active or because they do not understand themselves or their destinies yet.

Some peoples egos organize their physical behaviour so that they are strong in the world whereas others people may be more effective through their training or the events they astrally create for themselves.

As our spirit grows in its ability to direct the flow we can be consciously aware of what we are involved in, in the physical world and spiritually, so that we can be awake in telepathic or astral activities to some extent as well.

Tribal groups wishing to initiate new members, used to starve them, prevent sleep and induce fear to lower their ego strength, disorient their etheric and desire bodies and open them up to being temporarily possessed by their group. In this way major changes to a person could be made easily. If we know ourselves it is possible to remain strong in our own purpose, even through ill health or exhaustion.

If we live out other people's requirements or expectations, we may not develop any self knowledge with which we can make our personal decisions to enable us to live in harmony with ourselves.

Our ego is strengthened by making constant decisions and pushing against opposing forces from our past and from other people. We may need to develop habits of exploring, choosing and asserting, as a means of strengthening our spirits until the process becomes a natural one.

Restoring our relationships to balance assists us to come to balance in ourselves and leads to personal empowerment as we can empower others by choice rather than through subservience. When we need support we can, without guilt or discomfort, accept the support that others offer through spiritual or physical realms.

When we relax, and cease thinking and creating new material to reconcile, when we limit our desires and the subsequent subconscious activities needed to bring them about, and forgive and restore harmony with people, we allow more areas to come to balance.

To be at peace with ourselves and the world enables us to be powerful through our surplus of available energy, and our support from our community.

Dedicating all of our resources to tasks and training tires us and makes us vulnerable but being without a purpose can do the same. Our egos can get lazy and forget to push out when we need to. Somehow a balance of being engaged with directed attention without stress can be kept. Some people are mindful even when still, by purposely choosing how or what to give attention to.

In balancing our egos we develop a positive confident approach to life. We can choose beliefs and aspirations which enhance positive relationships with everyone. With strong personal foundations we can rarely be undermined. As our spirits strengthen and grow we broaden our awareness and scope so that we can participate in more of life if we wish.

It is possible to be active in public life for the enjoyment of it or out of compassion for people and interact equally with all people as we choose, giving or receiving appropriate assistance and then letting go. Some people do not need the relationship to go any further, enjoying the moment as beautiful and complete in itself rather than as an opportunity for extending their influence.

A strong and healthy ego can enable us to be flexible every moment of our lives and out of our feeling of confidence and security we can be compassionate and participate in life in a co-operative way.

48 Discovering our Selves.

Our higher selves are the totality of our beings in connection with our community. Where our egos, in protection, are frequently exclusive of the forces of other people our h.selves are inclusive. Until our egos are strong and balanced it is difficult for our h.self to play its part in a balanced way. We cannot be truly considerate of others while our own insecurities, fears, habits or desires, dominate us.

If we become more powerful in our beings we can create chaos for everyone unless we have already brought our own forces into harmony with our communities where ever possible. Bringing our own forces to harmony while learning to expand our acceptance to a diversity of positive influences we enable ourselves to open up further to our communities without being overwhelmed.

By maintaining our health, by choosing and creating our personal foundations, by nurturing our soul qualities, by coming to self knowledge and learning discernment, by remaining in harmony with the groups of our choice, we empower ourselves so that we can live in the world with self confidence without being undermined more than briefly or in trivial ways that we may initially fail to notice.

Whether we choose to or not we all accept influences from people we are connected to. This can be an enriching experience as it enables us to become a full flavored person with broadranging access to possibilities.

Dr Faustus opened up too far to creative influences and his life became a struggle to maintain his independence from them. If an individual wishes to be great, famous or play a public role, he often needs the support of many people each of whom may have their own agenda for him. The powerful, whether they are aware of it or not, attract more powerful supporters who may be demanding in return.

All people with community roles are forced to struggle to maintain their selves and their positions of integrity because if they haven't developed their ego far enough they can be spiritually taken over by their supporters or group.

To attempt to cut ourselves off from influences is also to cut ourselves off from support and prevents the flow of life from flowing through our beings, denying us the possibility of coming to harmony or oneness with our communities, or of playing an active role in it.

To be fixed in our beliefs and agendas is a form of protection, and a valuable one for difficult periods of our lives. In wisdom, we can gradually abandon many of our parameters as we come to act in consciousness instead.

Until we have a healthy spirit and soul our h.self may remain undiscovered. If people are overwhelmed by life, their awareness shrinks so that they "lose" themselves and act from their physical or unconscious needs. Their responses may still be assertive and if the person has a healthy ego, still balanced but devoid of any conscious consideration of the world beyond their own beings.

We all participate in the creation of our communities and in the evolution of our groupsouls and groupminds. Each moment of our lives we can be interacting with the flow that is passing through us, adjusting it in some way, or we can in harmony, accept or express all that we receive.

As we receive positive forces we can accept and re-empower them, while letting go of or redirecting any fears, aversions or negative thoughts. When we feel conflict between our forces and those of other people we can transcend the forces allowing events or new forces to arise that will suit everyone involved.

If we are fortunate, we may be able to choose with discernment, our thoughts, desires and intentions, anew every moment of our life. Alternatively we can set aside time to meditate or pray to enable ourselves to create a world for ourselves in consciousness rather than allow inappropriate forces to direct us.

In healing our own confusions, imbalances or negativities we create new forces that flow to our community, and in the process we contribute to the healing of the community we are in. This can occur completely spiritually, or it can flow naturally through to all of our actions and words and our relationships with people.

In discovering our selves we merge with our communities so that our own forces can be easily interwoven with the spiritual forces of other people.

If we merge before any development of our spirit and soul, it will be self sacrifice or self destruction as we may not have the ability or wisdom to appropriately assert our own forces to participate and enable our own destinies to unfold through all we do.

With self confidence we empower ourselves and give ourselves the right to participate in life rather than to be directed by others. While self confidence is based on knowledge and loving ourselves it cannot be complete until we also have a relevance to the needs of our community.

Merging with a community is two way, where we share our forces with other people and contribute possibilities to our communities events and development as well as being open and vulnerable to the forces available. This is only possible to do safely when we know ourselves well enough to be able to choose the valuable and transcend the rest. We need to be confident that we will always survive and prosper despite any disparity between our own forces and our communities.

In coming to selfhood we will also become a leader whether we intend to or not. Our spirits will have an influence over everyone we come into contact with, in our own families or nation, and our spiritual forces will participate in any area we are interested in. When we learn to live from our selves we become able to share in our communities resources and to fully participate in all that occurs in our areas of interest.

CHAPTER EIGHT

CONSIDERING OUR

CONNECTIONS IN

DIFFERENT SITUATIONS.

Individuals acting in the world can act with the power of a whole group, as the rest of the group can give energy support and guidance with their minds whenever necessary. It is possible for people to cooperate with their actions or their thoughts or both. We can constantly interchange roles with other people, from acting in the world with their support and while considering their suggestions, to directing or guiding them spiritually, while they are engaged in challenging activities.

49 Feeling out our connections when meeting people.

When we have established a habitual connection, it is as if the person, or object, has a permanent place within us which we can easily find and flow through. When we discover new interests, we can become more involved in life harmoniously, through expanding our existing flows and connections with the people who are already members of our groupsoul. This can happen naturally without us needing to seek people or make constant choices about them.

Each member of a groupsoul, while sharing common foundations, may also be exploring a diversity of interests. If we wish to explore new areas of life our groupsoul will usually provide people for us intuitively, that we can share with. In this way we may be able to make peripheral changes to our lives while remaining in alignment with our group.

Through our connections we become involved with different networks of people as each person we are connected to is in turn connected to others. By becoming involved with new people in this way we can find people with a diversity of interests who all share common parameters.

The people we meet through our groupsoul will already have indirect connections to us. We may have been spiritually involved in creating a mutual future with them for a long time so that on meeting them we can feel our existing connections and feel comfortable with them.

Some fortunate people can feel at a glance whether they are connected or not. "They're one of ours". We share something. Once the connection and the person is accepted the relationship may continue without being questioned.

We can intuitively explore or verbally question people, to try to discover their nature, their interests or the groupminds they are involved in, their friends and relatives or their groupsoul. We could also feel out the suggestions of their spiritual guides or our own, their feelings about us and their karmas, or how they fit in with our goals and parameters. Additionally we can feel our response to their physical appearance and behaviour.

Our personal feelings and desires can be at odds to our, or the other person's, group's or spiritual guide's impulses or suggestions for us, so that we may feel the conflict at the time of meeting. With other people everything we are trying to do flows easily and we may have many fortuitous coincidences and intuitive actions, leading to our relationship blossoming.

Some people may require us to alter our destinies to too great an extent. Other people's forces create too many conflicts for us to deal with at that time, so that we may not wish or be able to be happily connected to them yet.

If we have no expectations of a future relationship and are secure in ourselves, we can communicate at all levels and then let go, as no habitual connection is necessary.

With some people our connections are as big and as open as rivers with a gushing flow of emotions between us at times and with others there is just a trickle. Usually the stronger connections are with family and friends but this strong flow can happen with a stranger and we know there is a connection immediately.

Some people we meet are forgotten immediately while others occupy much of our thoughts and imaginings for a long time. We can test the contents that relate to them to see if it flows out of who they are or only from our desires.

Sometimes in our thoughts we have called out for particular types of people and when meeting someone we may recognize them as a possible answer.

We might see the same person regularly or coincidentally, until they become familiar enough to speak to.

Having had them in our thoughts at times enables us to begin the connections before meeting them as well.

No matter how obvious a connection becomes we never have a responsibility to become involved with a person. Sometimes they may feel right without being so. Some people really want us to love them and dominate us into feeling as if we do. We need to know what are our feelings, and what are our obedient responses.

There are different levels to our possible connections. With some people we can be very comfortable because ours is a heart connection and we may share a lot intuitively. With other people we may share dreams which lead us to challenges in ourselves or with other people, so that our relationship is rarely easy.

We can choose the level we wish to be connected at. At the groupsoul level with everything happening intuitively. At the groupmind level with our common interests creating the connections. Or at the individual level where we happily explore all possibilities with each other independently of prior interests, goals or parameters.

50 Acting with the support of a group.

Individuals acting in the world can act with the power of a whole group, as the rest of the group can give energy support and guidance with their minds whenever necessary. It is possible for people to cooperate with their actions or their thoughts or both. We can constantly interchange roles with other people, from acting in the world with their support and while considering their suggestions, to directing or guiding them spiritually, while they are engaged in challenging activities.

If someone we are connected to strongly has a sudden need of energy or panics, our physiological mechanisms can respond as well, with our heart rate, breathing, and blood pressure, all altering for no personal reason, whether in support of others or in sympathy with them.

Our guides, usually other members of our groupsouls, can complement our natures and abilities. We may be strong in ideas and imagination but need boundaries occasionally which other peoples minds could provide us. We could be great performers in the world, getting things done very effectively but not be very inspired. By acknowledging this we could open ourselves up to guides suggestions from time to time to increase our range of options.

There are times when we might become vulnerable to the point of subservience or powerlessness, and other times when we are strong and confident. We can discover the power of our minds and abilities to control or support others with them. When we come to some wisdom we may see the benefits of mutual cooperation with discernment and permanent vigilance. We can open up to inspirations whenever they could benefit us and enable ourselves to be effective in a harmonious way, rather than push through our agendas single-mindedly.

As a part of a co-operative group or groupsoul each individual can be the director of their own life while still assisting and being guided spiritually by any other member of the group.

To a great extent the effectiveness of the spiritual cooperation will depend on whether the members of the group can complement or supplement each other. Where there are conflicting agendas the whole group can come to a standstill until some of the members leave, disconnect and cease all their involvement. Because of this potential for being undermined by conflict, many groups have a person who dominates and leads it but with wisdom there is room for democracy on spiritual levels as well.

Acting alone in the moment requires great clarity which we can sometimes substitute with a lot of preparation. Working as a group at all times, however, means that we can always have the full resources to assist us. People who are well supported are usually unstoppable in life.

51 Creating new spiritual connections.

We could organize our futures by drawing on different influences and events, and people that these are a part of, just like a cook creates a gourmet cake, selecting the right amount of each ingredient. We could taste ourselves and if off balance we could take the necessary steps. We all do this already with our selective choices of music, colors, foods, dress, entertainments, and books, naturally asking what we feel like and choosing how we will be affected.

Many people make changes naturally in response to finding a new interest or getting bored with an old one and their choice of activities and people may all be intuitive. Their groupsoul will participate in the changes with them.

Other people can purposefully choose new groups to be a part of, by finding new interests, changing jobs, towns or countries, visiting gurus, priests, pillars of society or deviant radicals, or they let go of connections to groups who's influence they no longer want.

We can change our lives dramatically, by choosing to create new connections that have no relationship with our old ones. By being a part of diverse groups we allow possibilities that live within us to gradually expand, enabling us to transcend differences with a broader range of people.

When we take the risk of involving ourselves with people outside our groupsoul, we need to be prepared to accept the challenges that are created through the conflict between groups, purposes or influences, that result.

In creating connections we affect what can influence us, and in letting them go we may allow a stream of influence in our lives to diminish and then dry up. During the time we were involved we may have made much that was available our own. Its essence can remain with us so that we can still resonate with people, through what we have developed within us while connected to them, long after we cease the habitual connection.

Connections can be created at different levels and can be from the head, the heart, of a physical nature or governed by a single shared purpose or intention. The different kinds of connections lend themselves to different levels of consciousness. Some people come to harmony with each other in many areas without speaking, while other people can confine their connections to a single subject they share verbally.

Our capacity to make new connections in consciousness, or through our interests, is limited by the personal foundations we have established for ourselves. By gradually broadening these we are able to consciously connect up with a greater diversity of people. We can broaden ourselves gradually, on our own with thought, or as a result of experience with new people.

The process of changing connections is multifaceted as our groups also offer mutual support and spiritual protection and have expectations of us. Some groups that we are part of may not wish us to alter our relationships and others we are interested in may not want to share with us.

There are many ways of making new connections intuitively. This can be as simple as becoming neighbors, sharing a common purpose or belonging to the same group, where our connection is indirect rather than personal.

Sometimes we need to be physically involved with people to connect to them. By sharing rhythmical activities such as dancing, sex, team sports like rowing or marching, we create situations where unconscious transfers can occur easily, and we can get to "know" the other person with time, without speaking. It can also be induced through listening to the same rhythmical noises or music. Where a common state of mind can be evoked, connections can be made easily.

Where two people have shared an intensely emotional experience, a powerful connection, which can last for years, can be created immediately through the event, independently of any benefit to either of them. People who are concerned about karmic interference stay out of other peoples lives while they are in trauma, unless they are certain they are in harmony with them.

Usually there is a balance between the conscious and intuitive methods of making changes where we step in consciously when things aren't going as we wish and accept what is available when our lives are going smoothly. In consciousness we can observe our intuitive changes and explore their implications and consequences. We can choose from what is already becoming available rather than trying to impose something completely new ourselves.

52 Becoming an individual through diverse connections.

Many people are primarily concerned with being in harmony with their group. In terms of freedom from struggle and participating intuitively in the flow of life, this is a very valuable way to be. However it is rarely a road to individuality, wisdom or completion in ourselves.

As individuals we may have soul qualities and karmic forces that are unable to be fulfilled within our existing groupsoul. The process of coming to fulfilment in oneself can be very different from the process of coming to alignment with our group. The group priorities of conformity and loyalty make it necessary for individuals to let go of personal forces and accept group ones. Individuals have to actively assert their individuality to remain independent.

To come to wholeness in our selves and to find the freedom to be independent, it is essential that we have a range of options to choose our purpose, beliefs and attitudes from. Each group we are connected to can be a source of guidance and inspiration and can enable a new or different set of possibilities in our life.

People, who's identity is defined through their group, are more concerned with ensuring that everything in their lives is consistent with basic group foundations or reference points, than with universal truths, wisdom or value. Experiences they participate in, or the aspects of experiences that they give attention to, are chosen according to their consistency with group parameters. In this way the integrity of the group is maintained and harmonious co-operation is ensured. It is this group mentality which is the backbone of any community or society, for without it there could be chaos and perpetual conflict.

Individuals can allow themselves to participate in any experiences and to give their attention to anything that may be present so that they build up their world-view from personal experience rather than group parameters. There experience could be from any group, culture or time. To explore, individuals need to have an openness or vulnerability, as well as the strength and confidence to be an individual in the first place.

On the surface there could be a contradiction between the different ingredients they accept as personal parameters or goals. By being prepared to suffer and deal with the resulting conflicts, real individual growth is possible.

By accepting the challenge to be an individual, people can eventually return and contribute to their groups with what they have discovered from their personal explorations. By allowing some individuals to remain independent, communities ensure the continued availability of alternatives in times of uncertainty.

To be an individual it is necessary to choose our parameters and goals ourselves but to survive as an individual we have to be aware of the positions of the rest of our community so that we can transcend their positions rather than oppose them.

Harmony between individuals can come through mutual respect, compassion and self confidence rather than from conformity. These are possible when people are conscious in the moment, and where a state of goodwill is normal.

A diversity of connections can challenge us to continually make choices. If we observe our minds, feelings or our behaviour, we could discover many unexpected changes that have flowed to us from new groups.

In seeking we initiate changes as well. We may have been conscious of the thoughts or desires that went out to others, but not of the journey of our forces or our involvement in organizing a response through spiritual realms. We may be conscious of the change in our ideas, moral values or state of health or wealth but not of how it came about. Each change in us has a corresponding change in our relationship with our world and will reflect which groups we are connected to at the time.

When we make new connections through our interests or goals we link up with people who may share a common interest with us but come from a fundamentally different groupsoul with different nationality, language, religion, sex, and customs. Our intuitive foundations will be different too.

If we are open to people from "out " groups we can be easily influenced and channel their forces back to our own groups. This could eventually lead to harmony between the groups but at first would be felt as conflict. There could be pressure on us by our groupsoul to reject the new people.

In a sense every time we share ourselves with others, with our thoughts or being with them, there is an ego battle between us and them, between our group and them or between our groups. When we connect our minds to people or guide them spiritually, we can influence them or they can affect us. If we connect with our higher self or groupmind we will be better able to deal with what we receive, as at this level we can be free of our habitual reactions.

If we are acting alone, we may often be vulnerable. It is usually only the leaders or initiates who have clarified themselves in every area, who are able to act totally from themselves. Even leaders may have inherited a successful pattern through their family or other groupsoul and can refer to them whenever necessary for resolution.

Members of groups assert their parameters habitually without understanding the basis behind them. As a result they may find it difficult to be tolerant of alternatives. Individuals, with diverse connections, can come to see the underlying value behind a diversity of possibilities.

In times of uncertainty we can use our intuitive feelings to test whether something is useful. Our feelings however, come from our past, our goals, or from our groupsouls, rather than from the needs of the moment. Discernment involves the intuitive receipt of options with our hearts and the exploration of them with our heads.

People who are confident in themselves can be more open to new people and able to make new connections easily. Someone with strong personal foundations can go out as an explorer into the world and connect up with whoever they find there.

Acting in consciousness we can be independent of the forces flowing through us. Acting as an individual, independent from any group, we can relate to anyone.

As we reach our personal point of balance, we can be more open to all of the influences without needing to be affected by any of them as we are no longer seeking, but observing. We can remain balanced through awareness and self confidence, being detached or involved as we wish, so that we can become the source of influences for others, enabling spiritual guidance or healing for them in the process.

53 Initial imbalances in new connections.

We may need a settling in period before feeling comfortable with new people. When we meet people who are too far out of alignment with us we can intuitively feel it.

When we first meet someone we can be excited about the possibilities with them so that they are in our thoughts a lot. They may appreciate us but if they are affected by our thoughts and desires about them, they might attempt to cut off because we ask too much and overwhelm them. If we understand this then we can make more effort at being balanced and mentally wave at them whenever they come to mind. When a person joins a group everyone can be affected for a while until they settle in.

When we feel that people are worth being with, or certain places are worth visiting, we may at first need to spend short periods gradually becoming familiar with them and then withdrawing to assimilate what we have experienced.

Some people enable possibilities that can cause us to completely reorientate our lives. We may have wanted something for years but be overwhelmed when it comes.

When we meet people with big agendas requiring support, we are rarely empowered by them unless we share their agendas. People who we may have little interest in, or who may not present themselves as capable, may still in fact, be very empowering for us. Some people have few needs or desires and always have an abundance of life-energy with which they happily support others. The people we meet who can teach us something are often very different from those who can support or work with us.

Once involved with new people we become bridges between them and our existing groups so that what we accept intuitively, can flow through to them and stimulate changes. Within ourselves we will also be challenged by the interplay of new intuitive forces. People who have broad foundations are able to relate to everyone in the world to some extent.

Dramatic life changes can be liberating but sometimes they can also be exhausting as they require us to expand in ourselves to accommodate the new possibilities and to come to terms with the diversity. At times changes can be very empowering as we may let go of much that is no longer needed.

By ensuring that we have a surplus of life-energy when becoming involved with new people we will be able to find new responses with consciousness, rather than react habitually. My meditating or relaxing in times of changes we empower ourselves to deal with the challenges.

We can live entirely in the physical aspects of the moment; We can focus on what we have in common; inspire common goals; or ensure that we evoke confidence and relaxation. When we make new connections we can accept the best from people and set the rest aside.

When we understand the workings of karma we can relate differently to the people we become involved with. We created or acquiesced with the meeting so with compassion and equanimity we can alter how we relate to them and to what is happening.

54 Reasons we may feel the spiritual presence of people.

Most of the people who visit us astrally are completely unconscious of what they are doing.

Once we have experienced something and we have learnt from it, the skill or response can be taken into our habitual body and operate intuitively, being expressed automatically when a situation arises. This is also the case with our spiritual abilities. Aspects of our being, can interact with anything we have created a connection or habitual relationship with. Through desires or curiosity, we can also find new possibilities astrally, to experience or connect to.

Through membership of our groupsoul we become involved in many spiritual activities with different people without ever needing to become conscious of the people or activities. There are spiritual agendas which can continue independently of events in the physical world. We can all be involved in exploring possibilities, or training people, in ways that may not be expressed in the physical world.

When we ask a question or have an interest in something we will connect up with people so that we can receive what we are seeking. It can be as if they are present with us as they share with us, whether we have met them physically or not.

In consciousness we can visit people astrally ourselves or call them out into other realms to work with them or to be assisted by them. For most people, who have not awakened to spiritual realms, these things happen completely intuitively. Even after being able to be conscious spiritually there will be many times when we still operate intuitively and not realize we are visiting other people astrally or involving ourselves in their lives. Sometimes we may be conscious that something has been going on between us and other people but not be sure what.

When people think of us we can feel the connection with them. When they have a desire which relates to us, even if only a curiosity to see who we are, where we are, who we are with, or what we are doing, then it can be as if they are present observing us. We can be disconcerted by this or come to take it for granted and observe or ignore it.

From these innocent astral contacts often comes the beginnings of spiritual cooperation as the people astrally present begin to participate in whatever we are attempting to do. If our projects are of sufficient interest many people will become involved, through their curiosity or desire to be of assistance, whether we ask for it or not.

Frequently we set ourselves up by impressing people, or attempting to, so that they have an interest in us after we have left. If we are finding all the astral visits difficult we can ensure we don't do or say anything that creates worry or intense curiosity about us in others.

If someone we know is worried about us, we may have their whole prayer group visiting astrally or harassing us with their thoughts constantly. Where a less conscious person may deal with it all intuitively we may in consciousness respond inappropriately or find it unpleasant.

It may be best not to discuss our spiritual experiences with people who we aren't sure of as we can trigger off many rumours, curiosity and even spiritual games as other people may wish to show us what they can do astrally or etherically. People who are astrally present are usually like children, either silently observing or full of news to tell or questions to ask, with little consideration about whether it is a good time to speak to us.

When we are aware of the astral presence of other people, the level of our relationship with them can change dramatically for both of our benefits.

What we do, feel or think, while being astrally observed affects the person who is astrally present and our relationship with them. We can choose what to do while they are focused on us or disregard them. Similarly their presence can have an effect on us, particularly if they have fixed ideas about how we can be helped or who we are.

If we present ourselves as available sexually, people may include us in their sexual fantasies and we may see or feel their imagined activities as if they are occurring.

People may be obsessive about us for many reasons such as, being their possible rescuer, teacher or future employer. In being clear about ourselves and our relationship with them, we avoid many difficulties. We participate in much that affects us spiritually, so that by changing what we create and put out to other people, we alter the effects they have on us.

As we begin to be conscious spiritually, we will come to notice the spiritual presence of other people more frequently. It has always been happening but we were not conscious of it before. Where before we automatically responded to them for our mutual benefit from our desires or trained positions, in consciousness, particularly if we are afraid, we may frustrate new possibilities.

With our every thought and desire we connect up to other people and pull them to interact with us spiritually. If we detect their presence, rather than seeing it as them interfering, we can ask ourselves whether we may have called them to us, directly or through an interest or desire.

People are connected to physical objects, mutual projects and to mutual people so that there are many reasons why they will be spiritually present. Where they are focused on us they may not be in our physical environment at all but we might be in a spiritual space together instead.

All of our neighbors, even if we have never noticed them, are in a position of noticing us and in curiosity astrally following us home, so that they can get a feeling about us.

Knowing the diversity of people who can be present spiritually, it almost becomes imperative for us to learn detachment, acceptance of them or to go further into fuller clairvoyance where we can have a complete spiritual involvement with them whenever we choose or need to.

55 Entering a building or village.

Almost every place I enter, will have someone spiritually connected to it. In some way they will be claiming it as their own with their own expectations and interest in what happens there. The connection may be very strong and controlling, tending to direct people to appropriate behaviour, or loose and curious, observing who is passing.

Our level of familiarity or relatedness with each place differs and we identify differently with everything that we are connected to. At the point that our relationship changes with a place there is a border that can be spiritually perceived. There is a threshold at the edge of each room, house, property, town, state and country so that people moving through will be affected differently as they go.

The level of our protection and support changes as well. Children or adults who are yet to develop their personal ego, or not have incarnated completely yet, may be unable to separate who they are from their group and it may not be possible for them to leave their designated area with any comfort.

Group oriented people may have a whole series of rituals about passing through thresholds as their relationships change with each location. They may be forced, after going past the boundaries of their communities influence, to stand on their own feet without spiritual protection in a way that they would not normally do.

As we enter the town limits of a well established small community or cross a bridge from one part of a town to another, it is possible to feel the difference and to feel the observation and influence of the groupsoul or master dwelling in that community. Respecting this we can pause to mentally state our position and intention, verbally with our thoughts or imaginatively, or in conversation with the first people we meet, and wait to be acknowledged. We may over the next moments or days feel ourselves being assisted or supported in all we do.

The actual line marking "our" village can be down to inches with a town gate or welcoming sign as the boundary which everyone in the town knows and claims as theirs. This is still the case with old fashioned towns in modern countries. We can feel this change in foreign countries as well as it is independent of language. To a large extent what is being felt out is our attitude and focus of attention, and what is being evoked in us is a state of mind.

Towns which are more developed or have a high turnover of people may have much of their territory as foreign ground, that people can do as they wish on, and then some places which are very much for the locals as their own. Here they can feel connected without having to be involved in the influence or activities of what are frequently more powerful tourists.

When there is a strong connection to a building someone will intuitively come down to check on any strangers there. This connection is not as common today with public buildings such as schools only strongly linked to a proud headmaster who "owns" the place or a janitor who feels it is his to look after. Many other people, even if they work there every day, may limit their connection to the space around their own desk or room.

Some people feel responsible for their street or town so that their awareness is always connected to it and they may create many forms to protect it, and impulses for the residents to make changes. As they walk through they may with their thoughts suggest and criticise, affecting the energy patterning, and leaving directions for everyone who is open.

A place is affected by every person who enters it, and

whatever occurs there, but many people are receptive to what is available and do not impose anything new while others alter every place they walk through, intuitively directing their community as they do so. Some communities, like most of the Balinese ones, have specially designated people, often young girls and priests, who regularly go around buildings, doorways and shrines, restoring harmony with their religious practises.

Sacred buildings can be valued for the state of mind they create and their place in the social fabric. During good times the buildings are empowered by the people so that during difficult times people can come to use them as sanctuaries, to be restored or fortified by the energy of the building and the states of mind they evoke.

This sanctuary was traditionally the church but it can also be the family home as it often retains a particular atmosphere so that children, even after having left home, feel safe in it when in need.

The churches and temples, objects and rituals were fixed. Once the energy has been created and empowered for many years it is very difficult to change. There are many advantages of having everything fixed particularly if what has been created is positive and uplifting. However once a person has fully explored what the church and the community has to offer and has been transformed to being in line with them, it is difficult for the people to continue changing. The purpose was group harmony and safety, not individual freedom or personal development, separate from the group.

People who feel attached to any object, place or building are connected to them and connected to other people through them. As a result they are affected by the energy of the objects or buildings and the changes they undergo with the community that uses them.

Our roots may be to a village far away and in our thoughts and affection we could often be there astrally. To some extent we could still be affected by what is happening there, being supported in their times of plenty and being able to realign ourselves in our times of uncertainty.

Many successful shops may appear over staffed but the staff are creating an atmosphere of warmth, benevolence and trust where customers feel rich, generous and unconcerned about the size of the bill. When staff actively want the products they sell, people will be picking up strong impulses to buy and an appreciation of the product.

Impulses to buy are present in and around many shops due to the interactions of customers. This is particularly the case in book shops where there are always more good books than people can afford so they actively create desires for them. Impulsive people may find themselves buying the strangest books for no apparent reason.

If we enter a building or town with an aversion or fear towards it, we are psychically declaring war with the people and they may pick up on our negativity. Their response may be to attempt to gain our approval or to reject us outright. To enter a place with a detached, self contained, purposeful but appreciative attitude, means we will have minimal interaction with it, or the people who are connected to it.

The energies buildings take on and give off can also affect natural sites such as paths through the forest and haunted houses. Primitive people often had locations they feared because of something dreadful happening there. The event itself, the associations that followed and then the experience of the energies present, created or induced particular states of mind in people with which they empowered the site further in a negative way. If a bush path or road has been a fearful place it may get to the point where every person walking it feels fear and the place may be avoided at night.

Modern man has learnt, or is slowly learning, to direct their own attention at will and to develop a whole range of aspects of their minds that they can choose to operate from. People are often stronger within themselves and less fearful, so that they continually give out positive energy and they may be quite oblivious to the energy of the place or object they make contact with.

Our agendas are sufficiently strong that our moods or thoughts are not as easily changed by external energies unless we are open to them. Where we do have fearful thoughts we can dismiss them or laugh about them as being foolish, unless we are in an unusually vulnerable state.

In primitive societies a hero could slay the demon by remaining in the feared place and actively transform the energy by remaining focused, assertive and peaceful and not allowing any negativities to affect him.

We can purposefully alter the energies in our own or other people's homes and buildings, particularly at their thresholds if they request it. We can choose which states of mind to evoke, whether relaxation, reverence or efficiency or any other.

In knowing what is possible, we can be more conscious and considerate of the forces other people create for themselves or their communities.

56 Creating our own space.

Everyone, over time in a particular room using favourite possessions, colors and materials, can create a space to assist themselves obtain and hold a particular frame of mind, whether it is to study, write, meditate or simply to feel happy and safe. Other people entering the room would be affected by the energy to some extent and the usual relationships between the people would be different as a result. Even the weak can feel strong in their own rooms.

Many less secure bosses use props of their office and desk to assist them in having authority over their staff whereas more powerful employers and managers can create their own atmosphere through a whole building or in every interaction with their employees.

To have a room which is full of our energy is very helpful in times of illness, tiredness or self doubt as we can use it restore ourselves. If we are sick or vulnerable our old familiar clothes or the bed-cover we've used for years can be far more helpful than new or clean ones.

Where we have claimed a space as our own it will be difficult for burglars to enter it, even if it is open. Their attempted action would create a power struggle with our energy even when we are not present so that they would be reluctant to enter. If we have a strong connection with the room or house there is a good chance that we would be intuitively pulled back to it or arrange for other people to be, so that nothing unexpected can happen there.

If we live in someone else's house as a boarder we may need to assert our rights and affirm for ourselves, that while we pay the rent we own or claim the space and are masters over it. We may need to do this consciously and actively for a while until we feel it as our own.

If we do not own or claim for ourselves the space we live in them we may have difficulties in owning our own beings as well and be too open to trespass spiritually. In strange places we may need to take more care about claiming our own bodies and minds.

Any event that occurs in our space is affected by our parameters and goals and in many ways the energy present will reflect our spiritual beings. The events that can occur will be organized or assisted by all of our desires, beliefs, fears and aversions. As the space is ours we are the main person who determines what can happen there and people will need to be very powerful or well trusted by us to go against our will there.

If we are always confident in our safety and positive in our intentions our space will be a safe and enabling one. If it becomes negative or holds us back we may feel many intuitive impulses to rearrange the room to free everything up and to begin again.

To some extent everyone entering our space will fulfil the forces we have created for it. This can include members of our family. Many men who while working, spent little time at home, are dominated in retirement by their wives through the house. They may need to create their own spaces in which to be themselves or move house after retirement where they can create a new space together.

If we have long periods without visitors, then our homes can become saturated by our own energy so that it may be difficult for visitors to get comfortable. Where we continue to be sociable all our props can also assist us in being able to merge with the energy of other people. Anyone spending time in our space will affect it so that it can come to have a range of energies.

Our living space can become the sanctuary that we are spiritually present in at other times as well. Our presence can become habitual so that spiritually we can return there for many years after we have moved out. People using the space after us may find our presence distracting or disturbing so that they may need to change the energy and the physical props including the colors, carpets and furniture, so that intuitively we no longer feel comfortable being there astrally. We can do the same if bothered by the astral presence of others.

Sometimes it can be valuable to communicate spiritually with people who frequently visit us astrally, or get someone else to. In assisting them to move on to their new home or interests we can free ourselves of the intuitive conflicts their presence can cause.

What is available in a room will also affect the energy that is created there. The presence of water, earth, scents, food, oils, or unpleasant smells will attract different people to it astrally. The activities we carry out there, the objects we have in it, as well as our moods, feelings and thoughts all have an affect on who can be spiritually comfortable in our space and who will be able to enter it physically as well.

The value of having house warming parties can be in introducing all of the members of our groupsoul to our new space and in the process altering the energies ' so that our friends are comfortable in it at any level.

The energy of any place changes gradually by living in it and no consciousness of the process is necessary. By choosing to evoke in ourselves positive states of mind and experiences whenever possible we automatically affect our space in the way that reflects who we are or wish to be.

By creating an environment for ourselves that we are happy and comfortable in, we attract other people to it who feel comfortable in sharing it with us.

57 Taking over someone's role.

When we marry someone we take on our spouse's groupsoul and she takes on ours, or one of the groups may be intuitively abandoned to avoid conflicts. When we take on a job or takeover a business we take on the customers or clients and other employees at the same time. When buying a house we take on a neighbourhood and the previous occupant's associations with it.

The person who had previously been in our job had a series of relationships and had created expectations which may have become associated with the position. In the minds of everyone else it may be as if they are still present. In the mind of the person previously there, there would be many associations that brought them back to the position spiritually to interact with it and influence it. As far as everyone else is concerned the previous person may have defined what that role of teacher, wife or neighbor is.

Where a teacher has been in the one job and the one classroom for many years then it is as if they own it. They may have defined themselves through the job and still do so after leaving. They may still remember the children and continue their connections with them. The next person can be assisted by their involvement if in harmony with them, or possessed by them against their will if not.

The person leaving can take with them all the training and knowledge that they had accumulated while in the job. If they are allowed to be connected to the school, but at a different level, they can still contribute directly or through the groupmind whenever something they are familiar with is needed and they can participate in inspiring the school community.

Using ritual departures we can let go of the old incumbent, and all they are a part of, and bring in the new person with an acknowledgment that they will have a different style. This process may be over a long time, so that the person leaving is able to complete all their desires and redefine themselves so that they no longer intuitively respond. It helps if all existing clients are handed over by one person to the next, so that in their minds they easily become connected to the new person.

By reorganizing the house, job or asserting ourselves we enable other people to intuitively know that there has been a change. Unless we do this we may feel a battle with the communities expectations as well as the space we work in for a long time. Some people never fit into new positions or roles because they are unable to make it their own and come to harmony to their new community through it.

When everyone is aware of the difficulties of replacing someone in a role they can assist the person consciously and accept all the necessary changes as being their way of making the role their own.

58 *Being connected to our community*

It is possible to keep our attention narrowly focused in our own world or to spread it so that we can come to sense all the changes occurring or the possibilities being created over our whole community. While our attention is spread, who we are, will interact in some way with everything covered by us.

Some people's attention is unable to cover their own needs whereas others have a surplus and are able to be aware of, or support, the needs of everyone in their community.

When everyone spreads their awareness over their community it can become full of possibility and promise. Everything that is desired can easily come into being.

If ours is a positive influence we can enable our community and all that happens in it. Our influence will usually only be in the areas of our interest, role or experience. If we have a powerful agenda to change something in our community, that is clearly delineated, then everyone we are connected to will feel the impulse to assist us.

Using our connections with other people we create a meeting of minds, resulting in cooperation, sharing of possibilities or warfare. It can occur completely intuitively for all people, to completely consciously.

How attached we are to our community or geographical location affects how much we will be intuitively affected by what happens there. A life time association and "owning" of a community embroils us so that our personal changes can be totally intertwined with our communities.

If something new is attempted in our area we may resist it, as if it is us that is being affected. Anything entering a community causes the whole community to address it, to focus on it and deal with it, to incorporate or expel or defeat it. Most types of intrusions by new people or influences have a standard response developed to deal with them so that it may no longer need to come to consciousness.

A few individuals may habitually deal with changes on the communities behalf. Just as there are different roles in the physical world they also develop naturally in our spiritual life. Some people who may not participate much on a physical level, could be active and influential through spiritual realms. This is particularly so with the communities elders.

Our relationship with our community will determine how far we will be influenced by it as well as how much we will be supported. If we only have one groupsoul we may not be able to realize that other beliefs, ideas or goals are possible. If we remain connected to a separate groupsoul out of our geographical area which we can be supported by, we can continue to hold different positions to people around us.

The greater the range of connections we have the greater the range of possibilities in our life. Diversity enhances spiritual growth through conflict whereas familiarity leads to harmony with our community and greater involvement at spiritual levels.

CHAPTER NINE

NATURAL USES OF THE

FLOW THROUGH OUR

CONNECTIONS.

Once we have developed our abilities or knowledge in any area of life, we will intuitively be sharing what we have gained with other people naturally, without needing to be conscious of how. Our responses to spiritual contacts from other people, can come from an area of expertise or from the whole of our being, and be given harmoniously if it is useful. This is the case with all patterns that are a natural part of our being, or that we have created in ourselves, including those of physical, emotional or spiritual health.

INTRODUCTION TO CHAPTER NINE

For those who would like to start the book at this chapter I've included a brief description to prepare you.

We intuitively flow through our connections each moment of our lives, seeking, teaching, creating, learning, guiding, enabling, healing, directing, serving, leading, loving, sharing, and creating our futures. As we do so we work towards coming to completion in ourselves as our connections are the pathways for the unfolding of our karmic forces.

All of our intuitive flows are a natural part of life which to different extents can be directed. Examples range from people in meditative states guiding and healing others spiritually from a distance, in a purposeful, thought out conscious way, to parents who remind their children to pray for family and friends, empowering the child's connections, reinforcing their groupsoul and opening them up to assistance as they do so.

My purpose in this chapter is to explore these natural uses of the spiritual flow between people further and to show them as occurring naturally all the time as well as being able to be developed further in consciousness.

59 Creation with our minds.

Most thoughts and desires are like seeds scattered with little chance of finding fertile soil. Wilful and emotional thoughts and desires may be directed and active, having been nurtured and empowered. They can at times influence people in their actions, beliefs, goals and self images, without their awareness and almost against their will.

There are many ingredients that can contribute to our thoughts and desires being more effective in bringing about changes or events that we seek. When thoughts are empowered by our will, backed by our training, beliefs, goals and group, and fixed on a definite outcome or point of victory, people may automatically play their part to bring our determined desire about.

When our desires are in harmony with the needs and aspirations already in our community, they will come about easily, without need of discussion, with everyone playing their part intuitively according to their own goals or training. When we try to impose our desires without consideration of others an ego battle will occur. This could be without the awareness of the people involved, but it will create tension and even exhaustion for the people affected.

Some people have very narrow goals with strong and broad-ranging inhibitions so that they are powerfully assertive but rarely cooperate intuitively. Other people have weak or scattered goals and few inhibitions and will even cooperate with events that are to their cost.

When distressed or excited our emotional intensity is heightened so that the assistance we receive may be more direct and immediate. This also occurs when we are single minded about achieving our desires with the energy level not as high but constant through frequent repetition of goals.

Every change within us is a force that ripples out into the world with a possibility of affecting others as a natural part of the interplay of life. How effective we are in making the world into our own image depends on our clarity and the suitability of the possibilities we create.

Our chakras, amongst many other roles, are also a kind of volume control or power regulator for all our interactions through transpersonal realms. When a particular chakra is overactive, due to our needs or desires being very powerful, we may make people uncomfortable as our attempts to influence them, may unintentionally be too great.

There are many levels of creating possibilities, from creating a pattern for participants in an event to follow, to giving people mild suggestions about possible responses. There are many ethical questions about rights to give suggestions, or to influence or to dominate others with our minds but people already do this all the time unconsciously or through their prayers and dreams.

We can do visualizations, affirmations or pray or we can attempt to ensure that each moment we are creating something positive with our thoughts and desires. As opportunities arise we can let go of unnecessary desires, fears, beliefs and other limiting factors so that these no longer contribute to the creation of our future.

60 *Parents as spiritual guides of their children.*

A child's Ego is predominantly in spiritual realms and at first they are totally absorbed in organizing their physical body and their relationship with the physical world. The child is not usually able to spread their attention further out into the physical world and over other people and events. There is a gradual empowerment of the Ego and an enlargement of its areas of confidence and involvement that comes to self sufficiency in adulthood, and continues all of our life. Most children follow a standard sequence of discovery with each step a foundation for following ones.

Parents intuitively involve themselves, when they are able, in the creation of the environment that the child needs to unfold themselves and to awaken into the physical world through. Events involving other people are often organized astrally with the parents. While away from the child the mother particularly will keep her etheric body, over the young child to protect and guide them. As the child develops their etheric body the mother can guide them astrally and as the child develops their astral body the parents will need to act from their egos to continue to give guidance.

As parents we are only a part of the spiritual dynamic organizing the events in the lives of our children. There are other people involved and the children themselves will increasingly have their own agendas.

When a woman becomes pregnant her own spiritual bodies are reorganized to accommodate her new role. Much of her attention will be away in other realms intuitively with the child cooperating with them. In a sense this is a form of mutual possession that some modern mothers may wish to avoid as it is a self sacrifice of their own possibilities. As the child grows older the mother will gradually reawaken to more physical or intellectual pursuits but this may be difficult at first as the mother's attention is organized to be primarily with the child, their environment and future.

It is possible that modern mothers, whose awareness may have developed further into the physical world, may be more able to keep their attention over both realms. This is not always the case and many modern children suffer from their parents attention being predominantly elsewhere.

Children attempt to assist their parents with all that they are involved in and they are a part of their groupsouls. When the parents are focused on their own tasks, independently of their child's needs, the child is also involved and may be self sacrificing themselves spiritually in order to be able to assist the parent. Similarly teachers can self sacrifice for their pupil or apprentice, or the pupil can serve them.

We needn't plan the events for our children as much as enable them. To know and believe our children are safe, capable, confident, and to support them in the whole range of what they attempt to do, provides them with the positive view and life-energy that they need.

To have an image of our children slightly ahead of what they are capable of, allows them to expand into it when they are ready, rather than imposing an old limited view which can hinder them.

A mother, free from worry, who thinks and acts positively in relation to her child can intuitively protect her child from all abuse or harm and can be fully confident in the child's development, health and safety. This sheltering may prevent the child from learning how to protect themselves so that most communities have developed stages of changes for children, through which the parents gradually let them go. It is this balance which is so difficult for parents with some letting go much too soon and others keeping control until they die.

Some children have difficulty " waking up " to the physical conscious world, or retreat to other realms when bored or fearful. They can sometimes be reached more easily with our positive loving thoughts than anything we can actively do.

This duality of realms remains with all of us with the balance tipped to the physical world as we become adults. Once we have mastered the physical world we can extend our consciousness into other realms once more. These interests, in spiritual activities are often reawakened naturally in our middle years.

A child who can trust life in the physical world, can feel safe in incarnating into it more completely. They can then learn to interact with the physical world more effectively because their attention can remain in it. Some children have the opposite problem of being pulled into full consciousness in the physical world too soon and being deprived of the intense nurturing they could have received while still focused in other realms. If children complete their awakening too soon they may not be properly prepared for what they encounter here in the material realm. This can cause them to retreat to narrow safe areas of life or to protect themselves excessively.

One of the problems of modern transient life styles is that a child often has few or no strong connections with adults. Their parents energy and attention may be dedicated to their work and related concerns. Their teachers are overworked and change at least each year. Other adults such as grandparents, uncles and aunts often live too far away for a strong connection to be possible. As a result many modern children have inadequate spiritual support and can easily become uncertain, confused or disruptive.

Parents, and other adult friends, can empower their children by supporting them with both their positive influence and their energy. They can dedicate a little time each day to the child, while together or while apart.

People, other than parents, can make powerful connections with children and continue them for their whole childhood or life, assisting the child with their positive thoughts, prayers and support whenever possible. While this may be very valuable, particularly in dysfunctional families, it often leads the child to conflicts with their family later in life as the influence may not be compatible with the family agendas or beliefs.

The adult who holds the child in their thoughts needs to ensure that their agendas and parameters are relevant, to help prepare the child for the future. To assist others we have a responsibility of keeping up with the best of the changing world and to let go of all fears.

An adult usually has developed their Ego to be greater than their personal needs so that they can assist others. A child is in a position of needing assistance. Some children who are unable to organize themselves do so more easily when someone has their attention on them in a positive supportive way, whether present or not. Particularly when a child is sick, exhausted or unsure, the mere presence of a positive supportive adult strengthens them.

As a child becomes stronger they will naturally assert themselves and push the parent back when allowed. If a child is having too many or serious accidents it often indicates that they are not yet ready or able to protect themselves, or are calling the parent back to them. It is common for young children to have their accidents while the parents are deeply engaged elsewhere.

Parents can step in and out with their attention, gradually altering their level of involvement, allowing the child to test the waters, while still being available to them.

61 *Teachers guiding their pupils spiritually.*

A teacher who has a whole class of children, or adults, can only do so much while in the classroom. When the teacher has the same children for a few years, she can establish strong connections with each child which enables them to work together on spiritual levels while apart.

When the teacher meditates on the child, feels warmth and affection towards the child, then a positive relationship becomes possible. Sometimes a short evening of meditating positively on the child is enough to notice a difference in the relationship the following day. As a result the child is more cooperative and the teacher more intuitive, imaginative or inspired about what the child needs to receive, on a physical conscious level, for learning to occur.

It is essential that the teacher sees any difficulties a child has as something that they are passing through, rather than stuck with. At any moment the child can let go of a past habit or blockage which was hindering them but this is more difficult if the teacher, or parent focuses on the negativities. They can almost lock the child in to the problem with their minds. Instead a teacher may, with their loving thoughts, present a range of positive alternatives.

If the child has difficulty in learning or when the teacher would like to supplement it, the teacher can explore the subject in detail while thinking of the pupil.

When a teacher prepares himself each night for the following day, it is as if they are sharing the subject at the same time with their class, without needing to think of them individually at all.

Potentially the class can come to make up another groupsoul with the teacher and can participate in everything that relates to them. Obviously the extent of this sharing depends on the quality of the relationship between the teacher and their pupils and the interest in the subject.

For intuitive teaching to occur there is no need for the two people to be consciously focused on each other simultaneously. When we focus on someone it is as if we call an aspect of them to us and the influence or information we share can go through to consciousness when they are ready, as with an answer-phone. As a result people often know a lot intuitively without realizing it and discover it when the time comes.

By focusing on a child we call them to us spiritually, so that they can share our thoughts and desires with us and perhaps become conscious of them. Being aware of this helps us to accept responsibility for our thoughts more easily.

By working closely with a pupil's intuitive knowledge we can enable them to learn far more readily. We are bringing to consciousness what is already present rather than starting afresh each time. When we try to impart learning that we aren't familiar with ourselves it won't be as effective, as there is no possibility for the intuitive flows to occur.

When we have a habit of planting seeds of interests in the child each year, she will connect up with them and intuitively explore what is available. By the time we are prepared to teach more, she will already intuitively know much of it and will be hungry to bring what she has learned intuitively, to consciousness.

When a teacher has rapport with a pupil, the process of teaching through other realms is automatic. It could be taken for granted unless both teacher and pupil have completely disciplined minds. They would need to ensure that they never think about each other unless together, and have overcome or completed their needs to teach or learn. When they share a common interest and focus of attention this flow between them may still be automatic, even if they never think of each other.

When there is a close relationship it is normal for teachers to consider the needs of their pupils while apart, at the end of each day for example. It is a way of preparing them both for the new day or further learning. Any education system which is curriculum based rather than child or pupil based may omit this vital avenue for learning.

In the pre-adolescent pupil the learning is groupsoul based, where the pupil accepts all that they are told by people in authority on trust. They learn through their relationship with their teacher and group. When the teacher works with confidence, authority and enthusiasm, what they have to offer will be easily accepted by children.

When people are taught without habitual connections being made first, and if the material is presented in a technical way, then it needs to be worked with by the listener. This is an ego activity, to try to discern the valuable, that most children are not really ready for.

The essential truths taken in, in our early years become the foundations for later learning. Where foundations are in place and the subject is open ended, the child will usually have a natural interest in learning further. If there is confusion in what has been learnt, later learning at a higher level can be frustrated, until any learning in that field can become a chore that the child and adult will naturally avoid.

Allowing students their talents, abilities and interests to unfold naturally enables them to be clear in themselves about all that they are involved in. When they need to know more later in life, the clarity of the learning will enable them to tap into the groupmind to explore further.

A child's learning at school can begin with the foundations that have already been learnt with their mother or carer. We are spiritually saturated with all that goes on in our families and have learnt much intuitively that can become our foundation knowledge and experience in new areas.

Some people learn best from actual experiences while others operate best from thought or images and metaphors.

This is also the case with some children who don't learn much directly from what is operated on physically in the classroom, but who absorb by a kind of spiritual osmosis what they need from the rest of the group. How well these children learn depends on the quality or atmosphere of the group they are in rather than the content of any lessons.

When a teacher has developed her spiritual consciousness sufficiently she may be aware of the progress of her pupil and have no need for physical contact and guide the learning or unfolding of her pupil, whether adult or child, daily for many years. The pupil may forget her relationship to the teacher but occasionally be aware that she has come to understand those thing she once aimed to.

We can have the same experiences endlessly and perhaps to our sorrow, without finding our way to deal with then or avoid them in future. By having someone directing our attention to the ingredients of the events or the process we can come to understand them.

An art teacher may have high hopes for a pupil so that she focuses on her frequently while apart and has suggestions for her. Intuitively she may even know what her pupil is exploring and be guiding her by turning her head or noticing books or artworks and evoking enthusiasm for them. At times the teachers involvement may be so strong that it is as if she is guiding her pupils hands automatically, as well as her choice of materials.

A teacher and their pupils could be sharing artistic influences, interests, passions and techniques from a distance, perhaps as they meet astrally at night, which the pupils can put into practise themselves the next day. In this way the pupil can be assisted through difficulties and inspired to new possibilities.

All true teachers have a continuing relationship with their pupils. Where it is a genuine teacher-pupil relationship there will be a strong connection for support and influence to flow through. By a teacher taking care in what they focus their attention on while also focused on the pupil, she can choose what to transmit.

It is possible to consciously direct just what we wish to send out, even to individual people. Whole lectures can be broadcast, with the person being consciously aware of it; or remembering it as if they had a dream of someone speaking to them. Alternatively when the flow is too strong they may allow themselves to be a channel and speak the thoughts they receive out aloud.

Many teachers lecture people intuitively, simply by responding in a habitual way to a question. When they know their subject well, anyone who connects to them and asks can receive a valuable response, even if the teacher is not conscious of their spiritual activity at all.

If we have a question or problem that we desire an answer to, we can put ourselves into a suitable mental state, direct our attention precisely to our subject matter, whether a person, place, object, image, concept or spiritual force and then open up to what is present there. People we are connected to who find the question meaningful, and who are confident in their ability to answer, will do so intuitively.

62 *Using our connections for spiritual healing.*

Once we have developed our abilities or knowledge in any area of life, we will intuitively be sharing what we have gained with other people naturally, without needing to be conscious of how. Our responses to spiritual contacts from other people, can come from an area of expertise or from the whole of our being, and be given harmoniously if it is useful. This is the case with all patterns that are a natural part of our being, or that we have created in ourselves, including those of physical, emotional or spiritual health.

When a healer treats people in her everyday life as a health practitioner, her same remedies will be spiritually available as well. When her knowledge relates to physical or chemical remedies of movements, diets and drugs, then this is what she will intuitively advise others about, and in many cases this will be useful.

It is possible for healers to give all that a patient needs to them astrally or telepathically with the visit only needed to pick up the prescription or medication. Diets, exercises, minerals or vitamins can be discussed and recommended and people assessed and spiritually reassured without needing any further involvement from the practitioner in many minor cases. Before a person in need can be assisted by spiritual means, they need to be open to the suggestions or to the practitioner, and be prepared to make the changes.

In addition to the sharing of ordinary health practises by spiritual means, there are also practises that address our spiritual nature. It is possible to work directly with a person's chakras or meridians as well as to adjust their spiritual bodies, either while present physically or from a distance spiritually.

Some healing for our spiritual bodies can be induced through physical activities while other methods proceed completely at a spiritual level for both people.

It can be wonderful when the healer is able to harness life-energy directly and powerfully from the sun, or from the stars, the natural world around them or out of the air, or from their communities surplus, and make it available to an individual who is depleted in it. By having enough life-energy, self healing can occur more easily. We all have our own natural ideal patterns of health that we will return to whenever there is nothing preventing it.

At times a spiritual healer can link themselves directly with another person and dominate their patterns and tendencies that the other person has, with their own, clearing inappropriate ones and enabling health in the process. When one person has resolved a possible imbalance in life, their solution can be transferred to others intuitively.

Adjustments to a person's etheric body can be made directly on an energy level or through the alteration of a person's beliefs and habits. By telepathic suggestions, bypassing a person's ego, people can let go of blockages that they are stuck on. Hypnotists work in a similar way intuitively but while physically present with the person. They redirect their client's ego elsewhere first, so that they can make direct changes, without their ego protection.

A person's astral body can be stimulated or encouraged to unfold by giving healing images and suggestions and supporting their desires. A new self image can be encouraged that will enable better health.

Some healers, whether they intend to or not, allow a transfer of the imbalances to themselves, where through their own struggles, they transform or transcend the imbalances, enabling them to directly heal others from their community who seek it, in these areas in future. Other healers work as spiritual guides assisting people to reorganize their lives, so that health comes as a result.

The distant spiritual healing can occur in consciousness and a person can be taken through changes one step at a time. Alternatively a healer can work by focusing on a person while in a positive state of mind and believing that through god's will they will be healed. There is no need for consciousness of the process to be present for the healing to occur, in fact sometimes it can get in the way.

When the healing occurs intuitively, while the healer is temporarily focused on the client, the client is having aspects of their being brought into alignment with successful patterns of being, available to the healer. The client will be brought closer to harmony with the healers community so that other conflicts can be resolved intuitively at the same time. The healer can be acting as the bridge for his, gods, group or spiritual stream.

If a person has many fears or feelings of uncertainty, they are participating in the creating of negative events. By being connected to people who do not share the fears or uncertainties the forces, that were tending towards creating something negative, are disempowered or redirected.

Any person who is of a positive healthy disposition, who has confidence in life, will naturally participate in lifting the health of their community, in physical, emotional and spiritual areas.

When we discover we have abilities to affect people with our minds or spirits we can come to believe that we can save the world but cause chaos instead, so I am including a few cautions here.

People are often temporarily ill or off balance due to other needs or goals. Businessmen may enjoy operating with high blood pressure as it enables them to feel powerful and confident. To be a true healer we need to allow people to define their own state of health. To try to heal individual areas of imbalance can create as many difficulties as it relieves. Often imbalances are part of a coordinated whole that an individual has developed to achieve their own goals or to live their lives in their own way.

Spiritual healing often occurs between people who may otherwise have no natural connection. Any influence that occurs spiritually between them can cause difficulties unless the two people are naturally in harmony with each other.

When we become more spiritually powerful we may need to accept that our focusing on people can in itself be a form of spiritual warfare as they may find the flow disconcerting. With the development of spiritual abilities we need to improve our mental discipline and refine our ethical positions.

The images and suggestions that we wish to send may potentially be of value but simply by focusing on a person with our own agendas we can distract them from what they are involved in or create a conflict for them to deal with. Some people who receive unusual images or impulses assume they are going crazy rather than appreciate the value of the suggestions and can become demoralized rather than empowered.

Some people who attempt to do spiritual healing wish to send life-energy to support someone who they think needs it but by focusing on a person with more energy they may drain them instead. This frequently happens with beginners who inflate themselves while "healing" by thinking they are wonderful in being able to help others.

If people focus on others while praying or meditating and then fall asleep, a flow of their material may continue to be sent to the other person who has their mind filled with a lot of irrelevant nonsense until they can close off or get the person to wake up and change their focus.

It may be of more value to create a surplus of life-energy in ourselves through meditation so that we can make it available to all who need it and then leave it up to the "gods" to share out.

In bringing ourselves to balance and harmony with our community, who we are in ourselves can become a healing force without us needing to give it any consideration. By continually dealing positively with the conflicts that can arise due to the clash between our past and future and between ourselves and others, we also create tools of healing for other people, which they can take advantage of, if they wish.

63 Healing and creating harmony through a group.

When groups use rituals, or ceremonies, they often first evoke by the entrance rites and preliminary events, a state of mind where people open up to the collective spiritual influence. All the ingredients available may be used, scents, sounds, rhythmical chants and bells, and well known verses and litanies, statues, paintings and furniture, so that unconsciously or otherwise the people are all able to align their minds with the community mind and experience communion. When they are all focused on higher realms of life this could be an inspirational communion.

Familiar shared rituals enable everyone to operate in very habitual ways while focused together, so that their beings are free to be away in other realms together. The whole spiritual experience can remain unconscious but the effect on the state of mind could last a long time and support the participants in all they do. They could intuitively hunger for the rituals at appropriate times, to be renewed or prepared once more.

In the process of the communion the spiritual leaders are able to bring individuals to harmony in themselves or with the community and to enable their spiritual development. The communion is an active experience through which changes, including health and happiness ones, can be brought about intuitively and people empowered for the following week, or year or stage of life.

While communion can be used to be receptive to transpersonal experiences, it can also be used to direct forces elsewhere, such as in prayer groups, where a common goal or healing may be focused on, to empower and arrange it.

There is a powerful healing tendency due to the harmonising of imbalances that occurs naturally where there is a flow in any group with a common focus. Imbalances that are a problem for one person are not for someone else so that in group work, without any discussion, many negativities and blockages can be dealt with as a result of unconscious transfers between people. While this can be very valuable, it is also part of the reason for taking care in joining groups.

Rituals can be created which first evoke a positive state of mind in some members, and then this state can be shared around. Winter, loss, or change can be fearful experiences for everyone and can diminish the group. Through appropriate rituals the group as a whole can overcome the negative forces and move forward with confidence.

A group spiritual healing can occur spontaneously so long as there is present in the group someone who has dealt with that particular imbalance or blockage before. Sometimes the group has enabled the change and it is the leaders role to bring it to the individuals consciousness so that she too can believe it, acknowledge it and be healed.

Shared activities in groups allow people who are otherwise not connected, through their groupsoul for example, to become connected temporarily through a common focus of attention and come to harmony for a while. These positive intuitive ceremonies and events can enable fragmented communities to become more integrated and harmonious.

64 *Healing the energy of a place.*

Behind the physical reality we can perceive are spiritual patterns which maintain them. These patterns can all be subtly altered by the interaction with our personal forces. Every experience we have in a place, on any level, leaves an imprint or remnant there which can be felt or perceived by others. New places, objects or clothes often need "warming up" before they are comfortable.

The flavor of energy people are releasing or taking in depends on the state of their minds or spirits, which in turn relates to their activities, thoughts and emotions. The totality of our forces can be involved with the forces being created in the moment usually being the dominant ones. As we interact we can be affected by the place, having our emotions, desires and type of thoughts altered by the energy present there, or we can impose on it.

Colors, smells, sounds, rhythms, forms, proportions of buildings and objects all have their subtle effects on our state of mind especially when they are regularly experienced as part of a routine or ritual. When the ritual has been created to enhance maximum focus of attention, and interest or reverence, the effects are the greatest.

Even without rituals or associations with any past experience, statues or paintings can evoke a particular mood or way of thinking in us. They stimulate us to operate from particular aspects of our being. Unless our attention is engaged elsewhere the objects will have an affect on us as soon as we perceive them. If we are fully focused on our own tasks or thoughts or are insensitive, we may rarely be affected.

Once we have experienced the evoked aspect of ourselves we can find it within ourselves more easily each time we come into contact with the statue or painting. With time we can create the mood just by imagining or remembering the object or a representation of it. With a strong ego and practise, it becomes possible to choose our own state of mind any time we wish.

In Bali, and in many parts of the world in the distant past, some of the young teenage girls and boys and priests are entrusted with the duties of protecting their communities. Several times a day these people create within themselves a positive reverential state of mind and heal all the doorways, public places, and sacred locations. With their own beings they convert the chaos of the day and restore the location to harmony.

As the girls or priests go around even foreigners present can feel the changes occurring, when they are open to it. They say they are removing the evil spirits and feeding the gods and they are. Those who pass through or remain there will be subtly cued in to a more harmonious state of mind, to the benefit of their community.

Once in Bali, twenty years ago, I was in a bus which travelled quickly and recklessly until it reached a crossroads where there had been an accident. The driver braked to a halt and ran to the place to deliver a blessed offering of flowers. He took it all very seriously but did not change his driving style. From his understanding of the world, when the place was healthy no accident could occur there. The gods could interweave the actions of everyone and keep them safe, unless some other demonic force had been allowed in.

The lives of the Balinese people were still predominantly organized intuitively through their groups. Cases of individuals acting from themselves against the flow were uncommon. Then, every moment a person's life was also involved in maintaining the divine order and purity. Places of accidents were cleansed and focused on positively rather than having warning signals erected or new rules made.

65 *Healing with stories and myths.*

The essence of all that we experience is taken deeply into ourselves and gradually it is integrated and reconciled with our other experiences. At the same time the essence becomes part of our contribution to our groupmind or groupsoul. All that we take in to ourselves as images or patterns of solutions can become available to us and our community in times of need.

A story, myth or legend, when it has a spiritual truth, is a concentrated essence of many experiences, from many people, that can nourish us with every detail and can be taken in with little integration or reconciliation being necessary, as it is already balanced and complete.

Myths and legends may be based on real events but the details that are retained are those that have proven their value. Stories can have many different sources but to have power to heal they need to be avenues through which positive experiences can be evoked or be solutions to life's challenges. Stories enable people to have available intuitively a resource of attitudes and solutions with which to explore new situations.

The creation and handing over of stories was once a sacred affair as their value and place in the creation of future events, and people's response to different situations, was intuitively understood.

Each shared story is like an affirmation or visualization which is repeated endlessly by a whole community at different times in their lives.

The stories were often created, refined or empowered with the co-operation of the "gods" ensuring that they were relevant to the people, place and time. The often repeated and empowered sacred stories, once taken into the groupsoul or groupmind level, were the source of archetypal images and experiences. The ingredients of the stories were received by people in their dreams and experienced as omens in their physical lives.

The contents of the stories were alive in people's lives so that there was an interaction with them on many levels, subtly changing them. All stories, even the bible for the first few centuries, were traditionally upgraded intuitively, to ensure that they remained relevant and potent.

The beings we collectively share in our stories become some of the actors in astral realms, and the solutions become intuitive patterns to follow. They are available to us to interact with in an imaginary way so that we can incorporate them in our preparation of events.

In identifying with particular heroes, or being identified with them by our groupsoul, it is as if we allow that archetypal character to indwell in us for a while, and to guide that stage of our life. We can express what we receive in our physical life or complete it in our imagination or dreams.

While any events are still being prepared in the minds of the members of the group, it is possible to interact with them in astral realms. Many of life's challenges can be dealt with by the group at this level.

In the past, when stories were fewer and purer, people could act as the hero or as one of the other characters of their stories would act, and observe with attitudes or from perspectives shown by them.

When the stories are well prepared, refined and relevant, they are healing stories, enabling children and child aspects of adults, to be nurtured and guided by them. These may be available at the time of the telling or through the groupsoul at a later time.

Through our cultural interplays we create a range of solutions that enable us collectively to move beyond the problems of the past to explore new possibilities. Where our stories have been changed inappropriately they can lose their healing power at the collective level.

Traditional story tellers repeated their stories word for word for generations, to ensure that nothing of value was lost. Young children feel a satisfaction when a repeated story meets their memory of it.

Each story we have taken in deeply can be a pattern for an event in our life. It can organize our reactions to a situation as well as the event itself following a script with everyone knowing their part without realizing the source of their agreements.

The following of scripts could be naturally expected on an archetypal level but it also happens on trivial analogical levels. Mothers with a favourite book could name a child after a hero and then choose their children's friends according to the suitability of their names or qualities to the story. This organization can continue astrally without the mother ever physically meeting the people. Other people can come to co-operate, particularly when the name has obvious associations.

The events of any book, movie, song or play can be the focus for the sharing of minds so that different people can astrally or imaginatively live in them together, choosing and changing their roles and making new agreements to enable them to continue creating together.

Where a play has been rehearsed many times the characters take on a greater significance to the performers, as it is like repeating affirmations or visualizations. The actors can take on their roles and the events of the plays can be patterns for events in their everyday life. To a lesser extent the plays touch everyone who participates in them in any way, or is connected to the performers.

On another simple level, where a person has a single quality of a hero or villain, people create an expectation of the other qualities so that when we know their heroes and stories and who they see us as, we can know some of their intuitive responses to us.

The bible and koran read by millions, saturated the minds of the people so that they lived in them as if they were their reality. The collective consciousness of many groups were shaped by this involvement so that all behaviour and aspirations were referred to them. Due to their powerful evocative nature readers were able to reorientate their lives with the books, and collectively they reshaped the course of human history.

Individuals who saturate themselves with healing images become a valuable resource for their groupsoul. These images become a powerful part of what they broadcast to their world or spiritually provide in response to people's intuitive requests. Stories often have a far greater effect than thoughts as they are more easily assimilated and understood by people in need. They speak to a deeper level of our being.

To create new stories with spiritual truths we need to have an interaction with the people they are intended for on a spiritual level. The stories need to come out of our groupsoul, rather than our own thoughts. We can define the challenges and the people involved in them and possibly some indications of solutions. Then we allow them to taken over and interact on a spiritual level allowing the "gods" to play. We can open up to receive images in a state of awe or reverence but otherwise the stories could come while walking or bathing or whenever we have evoked the right mood of openness.

Our stories from the "gods" will have ingredients blended into them from all the people who have an interest in them and the writers may not notice the significance of much of it themselves. In the telling, the stories can effect everyone in different ways with different parts of value to each person. While it is the writers task to use discernment to ensure that only the best is used, when we have allowed the story to be created intuitively by the group, it can have a healing power for the group.

66 Co-operative creation of future events.

We may have impulses and desires that originate in our past, future or in the minds of others. When events unfold harmoniously we could claim responsibility for them or we could take the broader picture that the forces requiring the event flowed through us and that we participated in them for our mutual benefit. The flow of life continues through us all and we can share in it. We are all influenced by each other and act on each others behalf intuitively.

Our thoughts, desires and intentions are forces that are constantly seeking opportunities for fulfilment. So are other peoples. By choosing with wisdom, what we think, desire and intend, we alter what we create and the support we receive from others. While there may be struggles between people trying to get their way, eventually there are creative solutions which satisfy most people to some extent.

Each moment we are trying to satisfy a range of forces and to bring them to completion. Each event is a crystallization of the interweaving of the collective forces of the actors involved or those who have an interest in the event, perhaps far away or long in the past or future.

An event is an opportunity for a whole range of forces to be expressed, each individual flavoring their contributions in their own way. Each individual intuitively enables or delays the event until the moment arrives where it can be expressed in the most advantageous way. This applies to most events no matter how important or trivial, from the creation of a new world leader or cultural influence to the finding of an object we are searching for.

Our natural human curiosity and desire to assist each other usually insures that events, even if trivial, have a range of people involved. To some extent elders, parents, teachers and friends are involved in each moment of the lives of their children, members or pupils.

As we come to understand the creative process we can have more involvement in creating the dreams and affecting spiritual preparations, material outcomes and spiritual consequences. People who are organized in their desires, and ready to accept it when it arrives, can always have whatever they want. If we constantly change our mind, want too much or are in opposition to our community we will frustrate the fulfilment of our own desires and destiny.

Some people play the role of director of the play, initiating everything through the clarity and completeness of their desires and agendas, while others may be in the crowd scene or audience, doing what they can.

Understanding that we are all far more than what we express physically can assist us to address the spirit in each other. We can explore the totalities of people, rather than altering our opinions and friendships after each minor expression. Even if a person expresses something negative their spiritual forces may still be very positive and enabling and what they did, while being presented as negative, can have positive consequences in enabling the communities needs to be fulfilled.

By coming to understand our communities, their needs, habits and desires, we can begin to create with consideration of others. In this way we can enable others to fulfill their lives and gain their support for our own endeavours.

If at times we wish to alter the natural flow towards the future, because we have a view of humanity or the world which is different to our communities, we can with wisdom create the process by inspiring a new vision rather than undermining what is already present. My next book, details of which appear on the last page, deals with this subject in detail.

67 *Mutual empowerment of future events.*

When many people have few desires or needs, they can have a surplus of life energy and can enable other members of their community to complete their desires. If everyone in a community has many strong and opposing desires there will be great conflict, frustrating the unfolding of events.

By limiting the number of desires we have, we will be more successful ourselves and we will also be able to support others in their success. We can do this by letting go of unnecessary desires, rather than repressing or denying them. In denial our karmic forces continue, or are empowered further, so that we become more astrally active.

When we are a part of an event our desires will alter our participation so that we will benefit from it as well. If we have no desires or parameters in a situation we will intuitively act in accordance with other people's desires.

People who are well supported by their community and who's desires are within their access to power, always have an abundance of life-energy so that in their presence events flow smoothly, satisfying the needs of everyone involved.

Where there is inadequate energy, events can still unfold smoothly through the group collectively having the wisdom to find solutions to suit everyone. With an abundance of energy wisdom is unnecessary. If we feel a conflict it is possible to hold our minds still and allow our energy to support the person until they find their own solutions, rather than distract them with ours.

The flow of life can be in all directions with each person creating their own forces as well as perceiving and cooperating with those they receive from their community.

When we understand what the forces behind events are, we can participate in the performance with wisdom. Understanding the forces at work can also enable us to foresee future directions and to make longer term plans to affect them.

Our past forces continue but it is not possible to remember or deal with them all. When we accept responsibility for all that arises or passes through our mind and what we empower or disempower each moment we will be gradually refining and redirecting our personal forces. As we clarify our lives we will also become more effective and confident.

People who are confident, naturally influence others with their minds. People in times of shortages of confidence or ideas open up to suggestions. This natural mechanism has always happened unconsciously and has enabled groups of people to act co-operatively particularly in times of urgency or disaster.

People give and accept suggestions with their minds all the time. Many people have periods during their lives when they run out of dreams or hope in them, other people have dreams and ideas enough for crowds, with the sharing of the two comes the possibilities of fulfilment for all people.

68 About using Spiritual guidance.

A conscious spiritual guide is someone who has gone beyond the random flow and can direct their perception, thoughts and feelings precisely to particular people or communities, as they wish. There are people who can consciously perceive and respond at a distance so that we can communicate with them as if we are together, here or somewhere in between, and in a spiritual sense we are.

Some spiritual healers may assess a persons needs by communicating directly with the persons unconscious from a distance, and send healing images to the person in an attempt to stimulate self healing. In this case the thoughts of one person are sent out directly to the mind of another, focused both in destination and in content. This same process can be followed for any purpose whether beneficial or harmful to either party.

Spiritual guidance has traditionally been viewed as sacred, of angels, guardian angels or even gods, and it was seen to be of assistance to the guided one so that many people talk of trusting their guides or gods. This attitude was suitable for homogeneous communities who offered spiritual guidance and protection to their members but modern life is full of chaos and change. Protection and guidance that may be valuable and appreciated by one person may be regarded as spiritual trespass or control by another.

While we can acknowledge the wonder of the possibilities of spiritual guidance, it is valuable for each individual to strive to take charge of their own life, and to develop discernment in everything they are involved in.

To some extent, even without consciously choosing to be, all of us through our thoughts and emotional desires or responses, are spiritual guides to those people we focus on or who are focused on and share with us. Our intuitive or unconscious aspects are extremely capable. Just as we can drive a car automatically we can answer people telepathically, from our training, without any awareness or memory and most people do this every day.

Our desires in relation to people vary from wanting to serve or assist them, to simply be with them, to wishing to direct or control them. We may be curious but not wish to be involved in their lives at all. Whatever the motivation, any of these desires will lead our attention, consciously or otherwise, astrally to that person or the space around them.

When we seek guidance what we receive in response may be from people at random, from an individual who is conscious of their response or from collective aspects such as our groupsoul or groupmind.

For a person receiving spiritual guidance, it is difficult at first to distinguish conscious directed guidance from this random process that everyone is a part of. The first discernment needs to be about the value of what we receive independently of where it comes from.

As we learn to focus our attention and to define our questions more precisely what we receive will become more appropriate naturally.

A person receiving guidance may only be aware of it when they discover they have unexpected knowledge, skills, impulses, feelings, ideas or abilities. Even then they may rationalize it in some way, perhaps saying they must have learnt it subliminally or in a past life.

If we intuitively know a lot about a person before meeting them it indicates that either we have explored them astrally ourselves, someone has spiritually informed us about them or they have been connected to us and broadcasting themselves. Sometimes we can spiritually meet people moonths or even years before meeting them physically.

Our own spiritual guides could be our close relatives or teachers but could also be people who have a natural resonance with us, our purpose in life or a deep interest or love for us. We may have many different guides at different times during our lives and the people involved as guides may themselves never really understand the extent of their involvement in influencing us. They may be aware that they often thought about us or felt support for us but may not understand our receptivity to them, or how significant they were. Much of what they did or transmitted to us, may have been through the trained or conditioned aspects of themselves, rather than any conscious ones.

According to our own roles, allegiances, agendas, and morality we will attract guides to work with us. To some extent as we change, or our groupsoul changes, our guides will change to. It can be assumed that through our group-souls we will attract people who love us and through our groupminds we will attract guides who share a common interest or agenda with us. How valuable our guidance is usually depends on our relationship with our community and how well our needs are understood or agreed to.

Much of the guidance that individuals receive from their groups is intended to enable, or force, the individual to contribute to the community in a way that the community, or its leader, deems to be suitable. At the same time all individuals intuitively make their requests to their communities or to individuals in it. When we want something we may also think through how it can come about so that we can connect up to the people we include in our schemes. We will attempt to draw their participation, whether we are conscious of it or not.

When an individual is in need and lets people know their whole group can participate in organizing events for them. While this may be to their benefit it may not be to the advantage of people in the community who can be organized to participate. When we feel ourselves having unusual impulses or suggestions we can use discernment before going along with them.

We can use spiritual guidance as an avenue to rapid learning and achievement so long as we remember that everyone travels at their own speed for a reason. We can choose our level of involvement through other realms, rather than having it chosen for us by some " master" and maintain our egos and selves intact. While we can have problems because of our egos, without them we are only servants of an unknown master.

Spiritual guidance missed is like a book not read, it may not matter much. Some people, because of regarding the guidance as sacred, see it as always meaningful and vital to be ready for. What we receive are simply the thoughts and desires of people just like us. Some of them have developed an area of life further than we have so that it may be valuable to share possibilities with them.

The different types of guidance we have correspond to the different types of people there are, what motivates them and the talents or abilities they have. Just as we all vary in our talents, skills and senses in this physical realm our abilities in other realms vary too; between people and within ourselves at different times; after training or coming to personal clarity; or simply when we are having a good day!

Any spiritual guidance will only have a lasting effect where it is in line with the individual or is commonly accepted by the community she lives in.

Where people are active spiritually, other people or groups may adopt or enlist them spiritually to work with them. Some groups do all their training in other realms astrally or telepathically and in this way can work spiritually with people who may not believe it is even possible or become conscious of what is happening. Where we are strong in ourselves or part of a community it is very difficult to involve us in spiritual activities which are contrary to our interest or morality.

We may simply feel support, love or compassion for people so that at times of their need we may be present with them from within them or outside of them or felt as an angel standing behind them, intuitively perceiving what they perceive and able to offer suggestions.

Spiritual guidance requires an openness to it to be effective. With self knowledge and a well balanced ego we can sample from all the suggestions we receive from others whether we receive them verbally or spiritually.

Other books in the series
include.

Co-operative creation of the future.

Spiritual Perception.

Changing our karmas.

Preparing to be a spiritual guide.

Groupsouls and Groupminds

Creating spiritual harmony.

Preparations for meditation.

Life-energy flows between people.

CO-OPERATIVE CREATION OF THE FUTURE.
Another book in this series
Explores in detail,

SPIRITUAL REALMS AND ACTIVITIES. Unconscious spiritual initiatives and responses. The interweaving of our collective forces. Independence of minds from time and space. Logical and Analogical realities. Relationship of physical to other realms. The how, when and where of events.

PROTECTIONS FROM CHAOTIC CHANGE. Barriers to influence. Beliefs and Roles defining involvement. Rites of passage and harmony. Initiations and religious conversions. Rights to change the future. Value of personal foundations.

ABOUT DESIRES. Goals and parameters shaping events. Success in achieving goals. Psychic power struggles in preparing an event. Mutual creation of self image. Misfortune and its implications. Desire forces expressed analogically. Projecting our desires beyond our death.

REMOVING BARRIERS. Exploring personal limitations. Working with karmic forces. Letting go of old systems. Trauma, initiations and conversions. Changing groupsouls. Healing the past. Developing our selves, egos and souls.

INTRODUCTION TO
CO-OPERATIVE CREATION OF THE FUTURE.
continued

AWARENESS OF OTHERS. Sharing life-energy resources. Coordinating thoughts and desires with our community. Points of victory or travelling the path. Dominance, subservience, assertiveness and self sacrifice. ETHICS of creating events.

TIMING AND PREPARATION NEEDED TO MAKE CHANGES. Choosing our future. Having an earlier input into events. Weaving and seeding the future. Points of possibility. Timing

DEVELOPING OUR ABILITIES TO CREATE. Attention, creation, perception, imagination, intuition, inspiration. Exploring with divination and clairvoyance. Evoking modes of being.

PRAYERS, AFFIRMATIONS AND VISUALIZATIONS. How to. Who to pray to. Direct and indirect prayer. Watching our minds. Shared visualizations. Role plays. Affirmations, Spells and incantations. Choosing the positive.

CREATING EACH MOMENT. Guiding others spiritually. Stepping in and altering dreams. Acting intuitively. Creating a meeting between people. Choosing our involvement. Being part of the flow of life. Acting in the moment.